Deterring Fraud:
The Internal Auditor's
Perspective

by W. Steve Albrecht, Ph.D., CPA

Keith R. Howe, DBA, CIA

Marshall B. Romney, Ph.D., CPA

The Institute of Internal Auditors
Research Foundation
249 Maitland Avenue
Altamonte Springs, Florida 32701

ISBN 0-89413-117-6
84221 AUGUST 84

Foreword

Deterring Fraud: The Internal Auditor's Perspective will assist internal auditors, accountants, investigators, lawyers, and other professionals who have to deal with fraud. The authors have researched the backgrounds of many perpetrators of fraud and their fraudulent activities. Their research highlights the importance of having a formal program for detecting and handling fraud. Once fraud is discovered, it does little for corporate management to ask, "Where were the auditors?"

This book will help you deal with perpetrators engaged in "white-collar" crime. It will create an awareness about who they are, what their backgrounds are, and what makes them tick. Whether you *accept* responsibility for detecting fraud, as a control expert, you *are* responsible for safeguarding your organization's assets. You *are* the eyes and ears of your organization and custodian of its wealth.

In recent times, periodicals such as *The Wall Street Journal* have reported stories of embezzlement and defalcation where the consequences to the perpetrator were minor.

Some companies fearing reprisals from stockholders and a far-reaching effect on future business have taken little or no legal action against the criminal. The answer lies in better programs for prevention or greater deterrence of fraud. This study will *arm* the reader not only with practical tools but with firsthand knowledge of otherwise unknown case studies of fraud.

W. Steve Albrecht, Keith R. Howe, and Marshall B. Romney have done a superb job in compiling the statistics and case studies that make up this book. They were thorough in their research. On behalf of The Institute of Internal Auditors Research Foundation and The Institute of Internal Auditors, we wish to commend them for their contribution to the field of internal auditing.

C.W. Gissell, CIA, CPA
President
IIA Research Foundation
1984-85

Hugh L. Marsh, CMA
Chairman of the Board
The Institute of Internal Auditors
1984-85

Preface

Fraud has been increasing both in number and in dollar amount. A significant portion of our resources is devoted to detecting and deterring fraud. Previous research on this subject has been well conceived and has developed the basis from which this study grew. These prior studies have supplied a list of "red flags" or warning signals that suggest a high probability of fraud. Actual fraud cases were examined to determine whether these red flags are really effective in detecting and deterring different types of fraud. The red flags that appeared to be more important are identified and discussed.

We very much appreciate the help we've received from The Institute of Internal Auditors Research Foundation in conducting this research project. Its assistance in contacting internal auditors and encouraging support was invaluable. We also appreciate the contributions made by those auditors who participated through interviews and questionnaire responses. We want to insure all participants that every possible precaution was taken to protect the confidentiality of their responses. Results are presented only in the aggregate, and individual cases we have disguised.

Readers should understand that respondents were allowed to select the fraud cases they wished to discuss. Other than specifying the topic of employee fraud, we did not establish parameters regarding size or profile of cases selected.

The analysis and opinions of the research are those of the authors. They may not represent those of The Institute of Internal Auditors Research Foundation.

W. Steve Albrecht, Ph.D., CPA
Keith R. Howe, DBA, CIA
Marshall B. Romney, Ph.D., CPA

Altamonte Springs, Florida
August 1984

Acknowledgments

Many people contributed time, effort, and resources to the research described in this report. Members of The Institute of Internal Auditors, Inc., and staff – John Dattola, director of research; Rob Muirhead, CIA, manager of research; and Richard Holman, Ed.D., research editor, as well as Wanda Kenton Smith, consulting editor – provided administrative and production support. The Institute's International Research Committee, with Oscar Suarez as its project manager, provided significant comments and recommendations as our study progressed. Without the information provided by audit directors who were interviewed and who responded to questionnaires, this research would not have been possible. We are well aware of the time and the cost involved in providing us with requested data. We sincerely appreciate it.

Nina Abbott of Brigham Young University's School of Management provided a valuable service. She effectively and efficiently handled all the secretarial services such as the preparation of letters and their distribution along with the typing of this lengthy manuscript. We find it difficult to adequately express the true value of her contribution.

Bob Kellett of the School of Management assisted in the statistical analysis and preparation of the data. His advice and expertise were valuable aids in the completion of this study.

To mention all those who assisted in this undertaking would be impossible. To those mentioned and to the many others who must remain anonymous to protect the confidentiality of the information provided, we take this opportunity to express our heartfelt thanks and appreciation.

W.S.A.
K.R.H.
M.B.R.

About the Authors

W. Steve Albrecht, Ph.D., CPA, is professor of accounting at Brigham Young University and holds a Ph.D. from the University of Wisconsin. He is a former staff accountant for Touche Ross & Co. and taught at the University of Illinois and Stanford University before coming to B.Y.U. He has published numerous articles in such academic and practice journals as *The Internal Auditor, Journal of Accounting Research, Accounting Review, Journal of Accountancy, Management Accounting, Cost & Management, Financial Executive, Business Horizons,* and *The Practical Accountant.* In addition, Professor Albrecht is author of two accounting textbooks, a book on corporate fraud and white-collar crime, and a book on money management.

Professor Albrecht was selected outstanding teacher of the year at the University of Illinois, the University of Wisconsin, and at Brigham Young University and has also received outstanding faculty and research awards from the latter. He is a business consultant and teaches accounting and management courses to businessmen throughout the United States. He has conducted major research projects for the FASB, AICPA, The Peat Marwick Mitchell Foundation, and The Institute of Internal Auditors. Professor Albrecht is active in several organizations including the American Accounting Association, American Institute of Certified Public Accountants, The Utah Association of Certified Public Accountants, and The Institute of Internal Auditors, where he currently serves on its Board of Regents.

Keith R. Howe, DBA, CIA, is assistant professor of accounting at the School of Accountancy at Brigham Young University, where he teaches internal auditing, auditing, and government accounting. He received his doctorate in accounting at Arizona State University.

Professor Howe is a member of The Institute of Internal Auditors' International Research Committee and is first vice president of IIA's Salt Lake City Chapter. He is the recipient of several honors and awards such as the Deloitte Haskins & Sells Foundation Fellowship Award and election to Beta Gamma Sigma. Prior to his career in education, he worked four years as an audit manager with the Air Force Audit Agency.

Professor Howe has an extensive record of presentations and

publications, including IIA's State-of-the-Art Conferences and the Conference on Fraud. He is a member of the American Accounting Association, the Municipal Finance Officers Association, and The Institute of Internal Auditors.

Marshall B. Romney, Ph.D., CPA, is associate professor of accounting at Brigham Young University. He holds a Ph.D. from the University of Texas and is a former auditor for Touche Ross & Co.

He has published more than 30 articles in journals such as the *Journal of Accountancy, The CPA Journal, Financial Executive, Management Accounting, Journal of Accounting Education, Accounting Organizations and Society, Organizational Behavior and Human Performance,* and *Advances in Accounting.* He is the coauthor of *How to Detect and Prevent Business Fraud* and *1-2-3 from A to Z.* Professor Romney has completed four research studies, three of which are on fraud and is currently working on a research grant from The Institute of Internal Auditors on controls for microcomputers. Professor Romney has presented several papers at professional conferences and has given numerous speeches and radio and television interviews on the topic of fraud and white-collar crime.

Professor Romney developed training courses for Touche Ross & Co, IBM, Solid Software, the FBI, and several universities. He taught a computer-audit-software course for the accounting firm of Ernst & Whinney, a systems analysis and design class for IBM, and a CPA review class to unsuccessful CPA exam candidates. He also teaches a small-business-computer-counseling course for Touche Ross & Co. and an audit training seminar for AHI Associates.

Professor Romney is a member of the International Information Systems Technology Committee of The Institute of Internal Auditors and is also a member of the American Accounting Association's Computer Technology Committee.

Contents

Part 1

Part 2

List of Tables

Executive Summary

Employee fraud is a significant business problem that results in losses of several million dollars a year. Despite its staggering cost, very little is known about the types of employees that commit fraud, their motivations for perpetration, and actions and controls that can be taken to deter and detect its occurrence. This study is intended to provide information about these characteristics.

The methodology of the study involved obtaining demographic and background information on 212 frauds that occurred in the United States and Canada. The information was accumulated through extensive questionnaires completed by internal auditors in those companies that had experienced frauds. Data gathered related to the perpetrators and their work environments. The analysis consisted of computing frequencies of various perpetrators' characteristics, environmental factors, and determining relationships between the fraud factors in an attempt to understand the motivations for committing employee fraud.

Conclusions of the study can be grouped into five categories: (1) demographics of the fraud cases, (2) demographics of the perpetrators, (3) motivations for committing fraud, (4) organizational weaknesses allowing fraud, and (5) relationships between the fraud variables. With respect to the frauds, our major conclusions were:

- Twenty-nine percent of the frauds involved collusion, while 71 percent did not.
- A major control weakness allowing the frauds to be perpetrated was failure to enforce existing internal controls.
- Management's overriding of controls was an infrequent cause of fraud.
- Only 18 percent of the frauds were detected by internal auditors, while 33 percent were detected by anonymous tips.

With respect to the perpetrators, it was found that:

- Seventy-four percent were between 26 and 45 years of age.
- Seventy-two percent had been employed less than ten years with the company they defrauded.
- Older perpetrators committed larger frauds than younger perpetrators – 76 percent of the frauds greater than $100,000 were committed by employees 36 to 45 years of age.
- Perpetrators in insurance and financial institutions were

younger than those in other industries.

- Employees with higher education committed more costly frauds than those with lower education.
- Female perpetrators committed less expensive frauds than did male perpetrators.
- Frauds committed by males involved collusion more often than did frauds perpetrated by females.
- While a higher percentage of female perpetrators was prosecuted, males who were prosecuted were sentenced and incarcerated more frequently than were their female counterparts.
- Female perpetrators had been employed by their companies for a shorter period of time than male perpetrators.
- Only 51 percent of all perpetrators were prosecuted. Of those 98 percent were found guilty, and 31 percent were incarcerated. Fifty-two percent of those incarcerated served two years or less.

One of the major purposes of this study was to rank order the various factors that motivated employees to commit frauds. It was felt that, if motivations could be identified, companies could significantly reduce fraud by monitoring the associated employee pressures. The nine factors that scored the highest were:

1. Living beyond their means.
2. An overwhelming desire for personal gain.
3. High personal debt.
4. A close association with customers.
5. Feeling pay was not commensurate with responsibility.
6. A wheeler-dealer attitude.
7. Strong challenge to beat the system.
8. Excessive gambling habits.
9. Undue family or peer pressure.

When asked whether they would obtain more detailed information regarding these factors, most internal auditors responded negatively. The reason given for most of the significant (higher ranking) factors was that the information was of no value. It appears, therefore, that the audit directors were unaware of the correlation between these factors and the incidence of fraud.

The study disclosed that the two major factors motivating frauds are employee pressures and perceived opportunities. Several organizational weaknesses provided opportunities for fraud to be committed. The 12 most common weaknesses, ranked in order of frequency of occurrence, were:

1. Too much trust in employees.
2. Lack of proper procedures for authorizations.
3. Lack of personal investment income disclosures.
4. Lack of separation of transaction authority from custody of assets.
5. No independent checks on performance.
6. Lack of adequate attention to detail.
7. No separation of asset custody from accounting for assets.
8. No separation of accounting duties.
9. Lack of clear lines of authority.
10. Department infrequently reviewed.
11. No conflict of interest statement required.
12. Inadequate documents and records.

There were also several interesting relationships between the fraud variables. Specifically, it was found that:

- Perpetrators of large frauds used their proceeds to purchase new homes, expensive automobiles, and recreation property; take extravagant vacations; support extramarital relationships; and make speculative investments. Those of small frauds did not.

- Perpetrators who were intellectually challenged to beat the system committed larger frauds than other perpetrators.

- Perpetrators who believed their pay was not commensurate with responsibility committed only small frauds.

- Lack of segregation of duties, placing too much trust in key employees, imposing unrealistic productivity measures, and operating on a crises basis were all pressures or control weakness associated with large frauds.

- College graduates who committed frauds were motivated by their wheeler-dealer attitudes, close associations with suppliers, and overwhelming desire for personal gains. Those without college degrees were motivated more by the desire to take extravagant vacations, purchase recreation property, support extramarital relationships, and buy expensive automobiles.

- Perpetrators earning high salaries were motivated by their associations with suppliers, extramarital relationships, wheeler-dealer attitudes, and a desire to make speculative investments. Those earning low salaries were motivated by drug problems and the desire to buy expensive automobiles.

- Low-salaried fraud perpetrators were more likely to have a criminal record and a poor credit rating than were high-salaried perpetrators.

One of the most insightful aspects of the study was the actual descriptions of the frauds prepared by the companies themselves. These case write-ups are found in Part 2 of this book.

PART
1

1

Introduction

A growing concern for internal auditors is the increasing number of frauds perpetrated against companies by employees and management. Although many companies never report cases of internal theft, the FBI has labeled fraud the fastest growing type of crime – the crime of the '80s. In the one segment of business that must report employee embezzlements – banks – employee theft results in losses approximately six times as great as those from the more highly publicized bank robberies. In recent years, the FBI has committed approximately 24 percent of its resources – approximately 1,700 full-time agents at an annual cost of over $86 million – to fight fraud in all of its major forms. At any one time, the FBI is investigating over 700 cases of fraud and embezzlement, each involving sums exceeding $100,000.

Even more alarming than the increased number of fraud cases is the growth in regards to size. Years ago, if a thief wanted to steal from his employer, he or she had to physically remove the assets from the business premise. Because even money in large-enough quantities tends to be quite bulky and because of the fear of being caught with the goods, frauds tended to be small. With the recent advent of computers and complicated accounting systems, however, employees need only make a telephone transfer, misdirect a purchase invoice so that goods are shipped to a remote location, bribe a supplier, or manipulate a computer program to misplace company assets. Because there is often no physical possession of stolen property and because it is just as easy to program a computer to misdirect $100,000 as $1,000, the size of frauds has increased tremendously. Recent FBI's and Justice Department's loss estimates reveal the following:[1]

Areas of Loss	Amount
Computer-related fraud	$500,000
Bank fraud without a computer	23,500
Bank robbery	3,200
Burglary	450
Armed robbery	250
Larceny	150

With these increases, it is important that internal auditors

3

pay more attention to the possibility of fraud in their companies. Auditors need to understand the types of frauds that can occur, the motivation of people who become perpetrators, controls that deter and prevent fraud, and ways to detect their occurrence. Unfortunately, there are few clear-cut methods to understand, prevent, deter, or detect this crime. While many profiles have been published on murderers, rapists, and other types of criminals, very little is known about fraud perpetrators. While people who commit burglaries, robberies, and larceny are typically often repeat offenders with numerous citations available for study, many fraud perpetrators are first-time offenders with no history of dishonest acts. And while there are only a limited number of ways to rob a bank or retail business, there are literally hundreds of methods an insider can use to misdirect a company's assets. Most companies have limited their fraud work to establishing and monitoring controls and have treated each separate case as a unique occurrence that offers no insight to general deterrence and detection efforts.

A Framework for Fraud

Previous research has offered discouraging insight into fraud and related perpetrators. The completed work has attempted to answer the twin questions: Who commits fraud, and what are their motivations? Probably the most well-known criminologists to study the problem were Edwin O. Sutherland and Donald R. Cressy. Although their research produced somewhat differing conclusions, their complementary theories when taken together provide a possible explanation of the motivational forces that lurk in the shadows of corporate fraud.

Sutherland's theory of "differential association" is highly relevant to white-collar crime. He asserted:[2]

A complete explanation of white-collar crime cannot be derived from available data. The data which are at hand suggest that white-collar crime has its genesis in the same general process as other criminal behavior; namely, differential association. The hypothesis of differential association is that criminal behavior is learned in association with those who define such behavior favorably and in isolation from those who define it unfavorably and that a person in an appropriate situation engages in such criminal behavior if and only if the weight of the favorable definitions exceeds the weight of the unfavorable definitions.

Sutherland did not suggest that the hypothesis was a univer-

4

sal explanation of all fraud. What can be deduced from his work is that, where a company ignores or fails to deter crime, its action and those of the criminals working within and against the company encourage others to follow. When senior management of an organization engages in unethical conduct, accepts sloppy controls, wastes assets and talents, it opens the door for crime at all levels within its structure. Conversely, and this is possibly the greatest value of Sutherland's work, a company that creates the right climate of honesty can reduce crime. It can help ensure that the factors unfavorable to crime exceed those which favor it.

Although Sutherland's theory of differential association may not explain the lone embezzler, the generalizations developed offer further insight. Cressy theorized that:[3]

> Trusted persons become trust violators when they conceive of themselves as having a financial problem which is nonshareable, are aware that this problem can be secretly resolved by violation of the position of financial trust, and are able to apply to their own conduct in that situation verbalizations which enable them to adjust their conceptions of themselves as users of the entrusted funds or property.

From these theories and the results of our previous study,[4] it appears that three elements must be present for a fraud to be committed: a situational pressure (nonshareable financial pressure), a perceived opportunity to commit and conceal the dishonest act (a way to secretly resolve the dishonest act or the lack of deterrence by management), and some way to rationalize (verbalize) the act as either being inconsistent with one's personal level of integrity or justifiable.

Situational pressures refer to the immediate problems individuals experience within their environments, the most overwhelming of which are probably high personal debts or financial losses. Low incomes contribute to financial pressures; but gambling, stock market speculation, and expensive habits or tastes also cause intense financial pressures. Situational pressures can also be generated by strong peer group influences and even by official company directives to achieve unrealistic performance objectives at any cost. Occasionally, situational pressures, such as an urgent need for earnings or a shortage of working capital or cash, encourage individuals to commit fraud for the company rather than against it.

Opportunities to commit fraud may be created by individuals or by the company through careless internal controls. For example, individuals can create opportunities by increasing their

5

knowledge of the company's operations, by advancing to a position of trust, and by being the only person who knows a particular procedure such as modifying computer programs. A company can increase opportunities for employee fraud by allowing related party transactions, by having a complex business structure, or by using a weak system of internal controls. Anything that contributes to the capability of perpetrating or hiding a fraud increases the opportunities for it.

Personal integrity refers to the personal code of ethical behavior each person adopts. While this factor appears to be a straightforward determination of whether the person is honest or dishonest, moral-development research indicates that the issue is more complex.[5] Some individuals have developed a general trait of honesty that we call "high personal integrity," and these persons would normally be expected to act honestly at all times.

Individuals lacking this trait of honesty may or may not behave correctly, depending on the situational pressures and opportunities. Their integrity does not generalize across situations and is not internalized as a personal value. Their behavior is influenced more by the situation: the opportunity to be dishonest, the probable gain from cheating, the likelihood of getting caught, the severity of the punishment, and the perceived need for more money. Most individuals are between these two extremes – they generally believe in honesty but can be tempted by convenient opportunities and intense situational pressures.

The Fraud Scale

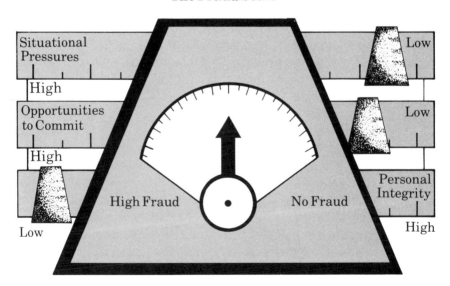

The interaction of these three forces is diagrammed in the exhibit. It shows a balance scale with three connecting top bars. Each bar has a weight that can move independently of the other weights in either direction. Thus, the combination of the three bars, along with the locations and sizes of the weights, determines to which side the scale will tilt.

These three forces interact to determine whether the person will commit fraud. A person with a high level of personal integrity and no opportunity or pressure to commit fraud will most likely behave honestly. However, the conditions for fraud become more enticing as individuals with less personal integrity are placed in situations with increasing pressures and greater opportunities to commit the crime.

In this explanation, all the variables contributing to fraud accumulate in each case until the force or weight is sufficient to result in the occurrence of a fraudulent act. For example, fraud could theoretically occur under any situation if a person is sufficiently motivated, even in the absence of outward opportunities or pressures. More likely, situational pressures at a personal level, such as a debt or loss, would have to be combined with a predisposition to partial dishonesty in order for a crime to occur. Pressures at the organizational level, such as the knowledge of others who have cheated or a lack of accounting controls, would also increase the likelihood of fraud.

Opportunities in general, or a specific opportunity in an individual instance, increase the potential for fraud. Further removed, but still relevant, are the societal variables that may provide conducive attitudes such as the rationale for a double standard (one at home, another at work). Lack of immediate punishment or the absence of threat may influence risk taking and dishonesty. If the individual has a strong, generalized honesty characteristic, he or she may theoretically withstand the.cumulative weight of all the variables described, although some will argue that "every person has a price."

With this explanation of fraud, it follows that perpetrators cannot be readily profiled. Rather, *all* employees are potential perpetrators; and as soon as the combination of pressures, perceived opportunities, and rationalizations become strong enough, dishonest acts are committed. To validate this statement, we refer to a previous study where empirical research was conducted to examine whether fraud perpetrators as a group differ from the noncriminal population and from other criminals. We compared incarcerated fraud perpetrators with (1) incarcerated property offenders (such as bank robbers), (2) noncriminals, and (3) fraud offenders on probation. Fraud perpetrators were defined for purposes of this study as those who were in managerial or professional positions and who illegally appropriated thousands of dollars from their employers. Utah state prison's computerized records of five years were searched, and fraud perpetrators fitting this definition were identified and compared with all other property offenders from the same time period where all the necessary information was available.[6]

Most criminologists would agree that incarcerated fraud perpetrators are probably not typical of fraud perpetrators in general. When compared to other criminals, fraud perpetrators are less likely to be caught, turned in, arrested, convicted, incarcerated, or made to serve long sentences. Therefore, only those with the more severe crimes and extensive criminal records are likely to be imprisoned. This should be kept in mind when trying to apply findings to nonincarcerated offenders.

Fraud Perpetrators vs. Property Offenders

The fraud perpetrators were compared with the property offenders according to demographic data (such as age, weight, marital status), criminal history (previous arrests, probation, incarceration), and personality (dependence, family discord, hostility, insensitivity) variables to determine if significant differences existed between the two groups. Means (averages) and standard deviations were calculated on all continuous variables, and comparisons were made by using statistical tests to determine if there were significant differences between means obtained by the two groups on each of the continuous variables. On dichotomous variables, proportions were computed on all traits for each group; other statistical tests of the difference of two proportions were calculated to determine if significant differences existed between the fraud perpetrators and other property offenders.

Many differences were found between the two groups. The fraud perpetrators were, on average, 15 years older than the property offenders. The older age of fraud perpetrators might be expected, since managerial status or positions of trust typically take longer to develop. Possibly because of the age difference, and in spite of the larger percentage of women, the fraud perpetrators were about 23 pounds heavier in weight. Whereas only 2 percent of the property offenders were female, 30 percent of the fraud perpetrators were women. (This previous finding is consistent with the findings of this study that showed that 40 percent of the fraud perpetrators were women.) A high percentage of women among fraud perpetrators was also found by R.J. Simon,[7] head of the University of Illinois' program on law and society. She reported that, between 1953 and 1975, the proportion of women charged with embezzlement and fraud jumped 300 percent. And she predicted that as women increasingly obtained jobs in positions of trust that allowed them to steal and embezzle, these rates would continue to rise.

Another very interesting physical difference is that the fraud perpetrator is less likely to have been tattooed. This is partially because of the higher incidence of women among this group but could only account for part of the difference. Many authors such as A.J.W. Taylor have found a relationship between being tattooed and criminality.[8]

The fact that the fraud perpetrators are older possibly explains why more were married and had more children than other criminals. In the case of the property offenders, 21 percent were divorced, as compared to no divorces among the fraud perpetrators.

There were also many social differences between the groups. It was found that, as a group, the fraud perpetrators attended school about three years longer. They were less likely to use alcohol or drugs. This is possibly because of the younger generation's greater acceptance of drugs.

The criminal backgrounds of the two groups also made for interesting comparison. The FBI's rap sheet of criminal bookings showed fewer entries for fraud perpetrators. Of all other criminal background traits that significantly differentiated between the two groups, the property offenders were found to be more criminal. The property offenders started their criminal careers at a younger age and were more likely to have been sent to juvenile correctional institutions. In addition, they were more likely to have escaped from a jail or prison or to have run away from a juvenile institution. A greater percentage had also been placed on probation. Consistent with the kind of crime committed by the two groups, the property offenders had a higher probability of using a weapon in committing their crimes, which were also more alcohol or drug related.

Besides faring comparatively better on many descriptive traits, the U.S. Bureau of Prisons' Office of Research has determined that fraud perpetrators have an excellent record of parole success. For those convicted of tax-embezzlement crimes, 95.4[9] percent were successful in staying out of prison after two years, a higher rate than for general offenders.

Differences between fraud and property-offender groups were also found in psychological traits, as measured by the Bipolar Psychological Inventory,[10] a personality test designed specifically for use with criminal populations. The property offenders were found more likely to invalidate their tests by their inability to read the answers, carelessness, or by making obviously absurd answers, possibly a result of their poorer academic skills. On all the personality variables in which there were significant differences, the fraud perpetrators' scores indicated better psychological health. They demonstrated more optimism, self-esteem, self-sufficiency, achievement motivation, and family harmony in contrast to property offenders who showed more depression, self-degradation, dependence, lack of motivation, and family discord. The bipolar criminal or character-disorder scales also show that fraud perpetrators had significantly fewer problems. They expressed more social conformity, self-control, kindness, and empathy when compared to the property offenders' greater social deviance, impulsiveness, hostility, and insensitivity to other people.

Identifying Red Flags

What all this suggests is that, as a group, fraud perpetrators are hard to profile and that fraud is difficult to predict. In fact, fraud perpetrators' profiles are more similar to those of noncriminals than to those of property offenders. As a result, the only possible avenues of deterrence and detection are: (1) to monitor the personal pressures of employees, (2) to insure that working controls are established that prevent perceived opportunities for fraud, and (3) to watch for behaviors that suggest rationalization of personal integrity. In an effort to understand the nature of these pressures, opportunities, and rationalizations, we have conducted several fraud studies over the last five years. To fully understand this study, we must review that prior work.

The major objective of our previous research was to conduct an extensive review of all fraud-related literature to identify the individual, organizational, and societal pressures, opportunity, and rationalization factors that suggest a high probability of fraud. Underlying this objective was the feeling that a thorough understanding of fraud can only be achieved through a comprehensive study performed by an interdisciplinary team of researchers. Accordingly, our past fraud studies have included individuals with backgrounds in accounting, information systems, organizational behavior, psychology, and criminology.

In reviewing this literature and other evidence, the following four data sources were investigated: (1) literature citations, (2) fraud perpetrators and victims, (3) organizations concerned with fraud, and (4) legal and organizational documents. In conducting the literature search, over 1,500 fraud-related references were reviewed including books, journal and magazine articles, monographs, newspaper citations, and unpublished working papers. With respect to the second data source, a number of perpetrators and fraud victims were personally interviewed. These included representatives from both large and small corporations, members of auditing firms, and both paroled and incarcerated perpetrators of fraud. Numerous organizations concerned with understanding the detection, deterrence, prosecution, or punishment of fraud were also contacted. In many cases, key people were interviewed and internal documents were reviewed.

The fourth data source, and certainly one of the more helpful, was the examination of legal and organizational documents. Donn Parker's[11] extensive files, containing over 400 documented computer-fraud cases, were examined in detail. In addition, numerous probation, parole, and prison records provided keen insight into the characteristics of fraud perpetrators.

As the data sources were examined, a comprehensive list of all pressure, opportunity, and rationalization variables that appeared to influence or be associated with the perpetration of fraud was compiled. Any variable that an author claimed was a motivation or prediction factor was listed. The identified variables were classified into three major categories: those induced by society, those inherent in the perpetrator's organization, and those experienced by the individual. Once identified, they were analyzed for content and factor. The results? A list of 82 potential red flags.

Some of the red flags were the type that would motivate employees to commit fraud against their companies (embezzlement), while others would motivate management to commit fraud on behalf of their companies (management fraud). While the red-flag list was only tentative and certainly needed validation, it is interesting enough that the research results are documented in several journal articles[12] and in a book published by

Prentice-Hall.[13]

While prior studies were extensive and the results well received, the main purpose was to develop a foundation for future fraud research.

Purpose of This Study

The purpose of this study was to analyze the red flags and rank them according to their perceived and actual importance in detecting and deterring fraud. In designing this project, one of the prerequisites was to determine the specific type of fraud to study. (The red-flag list was developed from all available sources and included factors related to management fraud, employee embezzlement, and even consumer fraud.) We decided to study employee embezzlement because it is the most prevalent and expensive. The following 50 potential red flags were appropriate for examination in this study:

1. Unusually high personal debts.
2. Severe personal financial losses.
3. Living beyond one's means.
4. Extensive involvement in speculative investments.
5. Excessive gambling habits.
6. Alcohol problems.
7. Drug problems.
8. Undue family or peer pressure to succeed.
9. Feeling of being underpaid.
10. Dissatisfaction or frustration with job.
11. Feeling of insufficient recognition for job performance.
12. Continuous threats to quit.
13. Overwhelming desire for personal gain.
14. Belief that job is in jeopardy.
15. Close associations with suppliers.
16. Close associations with customers.
17. Poor credit rating.
18. Consistent rationalization of poor performance.
19. Wheeler-dealer attitude.
20. Lack of personal stability such as frequent job changes, changes in residence, etc.
21. Intellectual challenge to "beat the system."
22. Unreliable communications and reports.
23. Criminal record.
24. Defendant in a civil suit (other than divorce).
25. Not taking vacations of more than two or three days.

26. A department that lacks competent personnel.
27. A department that does not enforce clear lines of authority and responsibility.
28. A department that does not enforce proper procedures for authorization of transactions.
29. A department that lacks adequate documents and records.
30. A department that is not frequently reviewed by internal auditors.
31. Lack of independent checks (other than internal auditor).
32. No separation of custody of assets from the accounting for those assets.
33. No separation of authorization of transactions from the custody of related assets.
34. No separation of duties between the accounting functions.
35. Inadequate physical security in the employees' department such as locks, safes, fences, gates, guards, etc.
36. No explicit and uniform personnel policies.
37. Failure to maintain accurate personnel records of disciplinary actions.
38. Inadequate disclosures of personal investments and incomes.
39. Operating on a crisis basis.
40. Inadequate attention to details.
41. Not operating under a budget.
42. Lack of budget review or justification.
43. Placing too much trust in key employees.
44. Unrealistic productivity expectations.
45. Pay levels not commensurate with the level of responsibility assigned.
46. Inadequate staffing.
47. Failure to discipline violators of company policy.
48. Not adequately informing employees about rules of discipline or codes of conduct within the firm.
49. Not requiring employees to complete conflict-of-interest questionnaires.
50. Not adequately checking background before employment.

In order to validate the red flags, it was important to examine actual fraud cases not previously studied. It was determined that internal auditors were probably the most knowledgeable information resource regarding unpublished frauds. Accordingly, the following research steps were used in this study:

• With the help of The Institute of Internal Auditors (IIA), numerous corporations that had experienced fraud and were willing to participate in the research were identified. To accomplish this step, the IIA sent letters requesting participation to 5,330 internal auditors in the United States and Canada. From these requests, 325 companies responded that they had experienced fraud and were willing to participate in the study either by interview or questionnaire.

- A questionnaire was developed incorporating the 50 red flags relevant to employee embezzlement, and participants were asked to assess their value. Because we realized that the effectiveness of our study depended upon the quality of our survey instrument, we spent a considerable amount of time in development and testing. After the questionnaire was developed, it was sent to the IIA Research Foundation's Board of Trustees' research director and research committee for review. After revising the document to include their subsequent recommendations, four different pilot tests were conducted. First, all three authors met with internal auditors from three participating companies in Salt Lake City, Utah, to review the questionnaire in detail. Participants verbalized their thoughts as they completed the questionnaire, and we were able to identify ambiguities and difficulties with it. Following the revisions, three sequential pilot-testing trips were made to Los Angeles, San Francisco, and Denver. At each location, representatives from three to six participating companies performed the same function; and the questionnaire was revised between each trip.

- After refining the survey instrument, we sent questionnaires to the 325 internal auditors who had agreed to participate. After two requests, we received 212 completed and usable questionnaires.

- The completed questionnaires were analyzed in three separate steps:
  1. We computed descriptive statistics on the perpetrators and their frauds. Perpetrator statistics included length of employment, sex, job title, marital status, salary, education level, type of employee, action taken against perpetrator, and length of sentence, if any. Fraud statistics included dollar amount, total recovered from bonding companies and perpetrator, time involvement, whether collusion was involved, condition(s) that allowed the fraud, and management's reaction to the

fraud investigation.

2. We computed means and variances for each red-flag question. With these means, we were able to rank the red flags by importance as they related to actual frauds and as they were perceived by internal auditors.

3. We correlated many of the demographic variables with the red flags to see if there were relationships between perpetrators' sex with amount of fraud, sex with age of perpetrators, sex with collusion, type of company with amount of fraud, education level with amount and type of fraud, and so forth. The significance of the relationships were measured by using Chi-Square statistics.

To our knowledge, this study is the first to delve into the information content of fraud variables. The exhaustive samples include firsthand information provided by individuals directly involved in investigations as well as their perceptions about the validity of the predictive variables. As a result, we compared common perceptions with actual case results.

---

[1]W.S. Albrecht, *et al., How to Detect and Prevent Fraud* (New York: Prentice-Hall, Inc., 1982), p. 23.

[2]Michael J. Comer, *Corporate Fraud* (London, England: McGraw-Hill Book Company, UK Limited, 1977), p. 9.

[3]*Ibid.,* p. 10.

[4]Albrecht, *et al.*

[5]H. Hartshorne and M.A. May, *Studies in Deceit: Studies in the Nature of Character* Vol. 1, (New York: Macmillan Publishing Co., Inc., 1928); and R.B. Burton, "Generality of Honesty Reconsidered," *Psychological Review* (No. 6, 1963), pp. 481-499.

[6]Albrecht, *et al.*, pp. 225-242.

[7]R.J. Simon, "Female Felons," *Human Behavior* (November, 1978), p. 12.

[8]A.J.W. Taylor, "Tattooing Among Male and Female Offenders of Different Ages in Different Types of Institutions," *Genetic Psychology Monographs* (1970), pp. 81-119.

[9]J. Prather, *Post-Release Success of White-Collar Offenders* (Washington, D.C.: Office of Research, U.S. Bureau of Prisons, 1977), pp. 1-10.

[10]R.J. Howell, I.R. Payne and A.V. Roe, *The Bipolar Psychological Inventory* (Orem, Utah: Diagnostics Specialists, 1972), pp. 1, 2.

[11]Donn Parker is a consultant with SRI International and is recognized as a leading expert in computer crime.

[12]S.W. Albrecht and M.B. Romney, "The White-Collar Criminal," *Prosecutor's Brief* (September-October, 1979), pp. 34-40; S.W. Albrecht, M.B. Romney, and D.J. Cherrington, "Auditor Involvement in the Detection of Fraud," *Journal of Accountancy* (May, 1980), pp. 63-69.

[13]Albrecht, *et al.*

2

Study Results

Demographics

The Fraud Cases

The response of internal audit directors was very gratifying. We received 212 usable questionnaires containing factual data on fraud demographics, perpetrator characteristics, specific causes, and audit directors' perceptions. Unlike prior research, our sample was composed primarily of fraud cases where the facts had not previously been made public. These 212 frauds were distributed across industrial classifications in the percentages shown in Table 1.

Table 1
Industrial Classification of Responding Companies

Industry Type	Percentage
Education	8.5
Financial	25.9
Government	5.7
Health Care	4.2
Insurance	13.2
Manufacturing	20.8
Retail	4.7
Service	2.4
Utility	7.1
Other/No Response	7.6

The higher percentage of cases in the financial and manufacturing industries might bias some of the study's results, so we will point out these possibilities where appropriate. The dollar amounts of the reported frauds ranged from 100 to more than a million dollars. Because of this wide range, the average dollar fraud was not as meaningful as the distribution of the dollar amounts.

As Table 2 reveals, our sample included a wealth of small frauds. Since it is probable that respondents would provide data on the most significant frauds of which they are knowledgeable, we could conclude that (a) most frauds are detected relatively early or that, (b) as internal auditors, we have not yet detected ongoing frauds which are larger in dollar amounts (assuming our cases are representative of known frauds).

Table 2
Dollar Amount of Frauds

Amount	Percentage
$ 1 - $ 20,000	45.9
20,001 - 40,000	11.7
40,001 - 60,000	8.8
60,001 - 80,000	5.9
80,001 - 100,000	5.4
100,001 - 200,000	10.2
200,001 - 1,000,000	9.3
more than 1,000,000	2.9

We did find, however, a statistically significant correlation (p-value = .001)[14] between fraud dollar amount and industry type. Note from Table 3 that 71.7 percent of the financial institution cases were less than $40,000, representing 32.2 percent of the total in this category. This result is probably caused by the large number of "unsophisticated frauds" perpetrated by low-level employees (e.g., tellers) who cannot handle the temptation of dealing with cash. Their frauds seem to lack any effective concealment efforts.

Table 3
Industry Type and Fraud Amount (percentage)

Industry Type	Fraud Amounts[1]			
	1-40,000	40,000-100,000	over 100,000	Total%
Educational	64.7	23.5	11.8	100
Financial	71.7	5.7	22.6	100
Insurance	46.4	35.7	17.9	100
Manufacturing	43.9	31.7	24.4	100
Retail	60.0	0.0	40.0	100
Utility	60.0	13.3	26.7	100
Other[2]	56.0	22.0	22.0	100

[1]For purposes of this statistical test, the amount categories were combined rather than using the categories in Table 2.
[2]For purposes of this statistical test, service, health care, and government types were combined with the "other" category.

---

[14]The p-value measures the significance of the correlation. The lower the value, the more significant the relationship. For example, a p-value of .000 means that the relationship is extremely strong and is probably not a result of chance. On the other hand, a p-value near 1 indicates there is no significance and any relationship is probably linked to chance. In this study, we used a p-value of .05 as the cutoff level between significant and insignificant relationships.

Sixty-four percent of the educational cases were less than $40,000 and totaled only 9.3 percent of the total cases under $40,000. The percentages for the utility and the retail industries were similar, although 60 percent of the cases were under $40,000. If one accepts the idea that there are no small frauds, only frauds found before they have large dollar losses, these industries may be doing a good job in identifying frauds early (or perhaps there are many large frauds in these companies yet to surface).

It is also interesting that, of the financial institutions, 22.6 percent of the frauds were in the "over-$100,000" category. These cases totaled 26.1 percent of this category. Only 5.7 percent of the financial institution cases were in the $40,000 to $100,000 category. Apparently, financial institutions' frauds are of two distinct types: those large frauds perpetrated by officers and management and those smaller schemes perpetrated by tellers and other operating personnel.

This same situation seems to be true of the retail industry. The frauds were either less than $40,000 (actually less than $20,000; see footnote 1 in Table 3) or greater than $100,000. The insurance, manufacturing, and "other" fraud amounts were evenly distributed (although the 46.4 percent for insurance shown as less than $40,000 represented cases of less than $20,000).

The length of fraud and company type were not statistically correlated, which was interesting given the relationship between fraud amount and industry type. A partial explanation might be found in the large percentage (50 percent) reported as less than one year in length. Logic tells us that a perpetrator would not admit to a larger fraud than necessary and that, once properly documented, the benefit of additional investigation to determine the total time frame diminishes. This is also true of the dollar amount. The large percentages of "smaller" frauds, both in amount and in time, should be viewed in the context of this argument.

Table 4
Length of Time Fraud Perpetrated

Time	Percentage
1 year and less	50.0
1 to 2 years	21.1
2 to 3 years	12.7
3 to 5 years	9.4
More than 5 years	4.7

The data regarding the length of perpetrator employment further supports the "no-small-fraud" theory. Table 5 shows that 40.6 percent of the frauds were perpetrated by persons employed less than five years with the defrauded company (71.7 percent less than 10 years). Although the cross-correlations of employment and fraud lengths with the dollar amounts were not statistically significant, there appeared to be some trends in cases over $200,000. They were typically perpetrated by employees with longer periods of service over longer periods of time.

Table 5
Length of Perpetrator's Employment
with the Defrauded Company

Time Period	Percentage
Less than 3 years	25.5
3 to 5 years	15.1
5 to 10 years	31.1
10 to 20 years	20.8
More than 20 years	7.5

The lack of significance of these cross-correlations requires additional comment. Although a large percentage of fraud perpetrators was employed for a short period of time, we cannot assume that these perpetrators were only involved in smaller frauds. In fact, the lack of a significant correlation between these factors tends to refute the "no-small-fraud" theory except that frauds vary in the rate at which amounts accumulate . . . some frauds build large amounts in very short periods of time.

When asked if the frauds involved collusion, 28.8 percent of the audit directors responded "yes." This percentage is probably indicative of frauds that were detected early in their lives. Collusion is difficult to detect because of the ineffectiveness of controls when conspiracies negate them. There were, however, some interesting and important observations regarding collusion in relation to other demographic data.

The correlation between collusion and company type had a p-value of .036. The manufacturing, insurance, and retailing industries reported higher percentages of cases involving collusion – 27.2, 40.7, and 50 percent respectively. The financial institutions, on the other hand, reported that only 11.3 percent of their cases involved collusion. This particularly low percentage might be explained by two facts. First, financial institutions accounted for 71.7 percent of the "smaller" frauds. One could assume that longer-lived, larger frauds might require collusion for continued existence. (We should note that the correlation between amount of fraud and collusion *was not* significant at the .05 level and that the p-value for this test was .075. The trend of this correlation, however, was that the larger the fraud amount, the larger the probability of collusion.)

The second theory is the nature of work. It is easier for someone in a financial institution to falsify documents, manipulate accounts, or use another fraud technique than for those in other industries.

Collusion and perpetrator sex was also highly correlated with a p-value of .007. Our study found that male perpetrators were more likely to collude in their deception than were females. Collusion was also statistically correlated with perpetrator-education levels (with a p-value of .002) and salary (p-value .007). The more educated or higher paid the perpetrator, the more likely was collusion involved.

The Perpetrators

A major objective of our research was to identify common personal characteristics of perpetrators that might help auditors identify potential perpetrators. In this section, we provide findings regarding perpetrator demographics; later, we discuss the importance of personality characteristics. We gathered information on several variables such as sex, age, marital status, length of employment, management or staff level, quality of work, salary, and prior records. Besides raw statistics, cross-correlations were computed between these factors and fraud amount, industrial type, and selected demographic variables.

The length of perpetrator employment has already been discussed (see Table 5). This discussion revealed that employment length was not statistically correlated to the amount defrauded, although some trends were observed. The age of the perpetrator, however, *was* significantly correlated with the fraud amount. Table 6 provides raw data on perpetrator age. Eighty-seven percent of the frauds were perpetrated by individuals 45 years and younger with 73.5 percent between the ages of 26 to 45. The over-55 category accounted for only 1.9 percent of the perpetrators.

When viewed in the context of 46.2 percent employed between three and ten years (see Table 5), we can conclude that the majority of the perpetrators apparently *did not* begin their careers with the company defrauded and had at least one former employer.

Table 6
Perpetrator's Age

Age	Percentage
25 and less	13.5
26 to 35	38.2
36 to 45	35.3
46 to 55	11.1
56 and older	1.9

As the table shows, the 36-45 age group accounted for 35.3 percent of all frauds. This group also accounted for 76.1 percent of those frauds over $100,000. The 26-35 age group accounted for 43.9 percent of the frauds in the $40,000 to $100,000 fraud category. Of the cases perpetrated by those younger than 26, 82.1 percent were less than $20,000; only one fraud over $100,000 was reported.

As might be expected, age was significantly correlated with educational level and salary. We found that the older perpetrators were more educated and had higher salaries. Even more eyebrow-raising, however, is the significant cross-correlation with company type (p-value = .001). Individuals defrauding insurance and/or financial institutions were younger than those defrauding manufacturing, education, or retail types. This may be because it is more difficult to gain a position of trust in the manufacturing industry. Furthermore, employees in financial and insurance industries generally have greater access to cash at a younger age, thus supporting our finding that both the sex and the age of the perpetrators were very highly correlated (p-value = .000). Also, male perpetrators were older than their female counterparts.

Audit directors reported that only 58.9 percent of fraud perpetrators were in "supervisory" capacities; the other 41.1 percent were classified as "clerical." There were some obvious significant correlations between this job-level factor and other demographic data. For example, supervisors were usually male, paid more, better educated, and defrauded for larger amounts. In contrast, the female perpetrators usually held clerical positions.

There was a curious correlation between job level and industrial type (p-value = .017): of those in the insurance industry, 66.7 percent of the perpetrators were clerical workers, while in all other industry types, the perpetrators were more often described as supervisors.

Just over 66 percent of the perpetrators were married. The married perpetrators were usually male with both higher salaries and education levels. They generally defrauded for larger amounts.

The education level of the perpetrators is shown in Table 7. Once again, significant cross-correlations existed with other demographic variables. Males with more education were usually paid more and defrauded for larger amounts. Of the frauds over $100,000, 52.3 percent were committed by college-educated employees. Almost 65 percent of the frauds over $40,000 were committed by perpetrators with a high school diploma or less.

Table 7
Education Level

Level	Percentage
High School Graduate or Less	52.1
Some College	16.1
College Graduate	25.5
Some Graduate School	6.3

Table 8 reveals the distribution of perpetrators' salaries. As previously mentioned, salary and education factors were correlated. Salary was also correlated with the amount of fraud. As a general rule of thumb, the larger the salary, the larger the amount of fraud. Perpetrators' sex and salary offered additional insight – male perpetrators were paid more than their female counterparts. In fact, not one female perpetrator made over $40,000 annually. Of those studied, 90.2 percent earned $20,000 or less. This is not to suggest that there are no highly paid female perpetrators but that the percentage, when compared to male perpetrators in our study, is very low. Of the males, 60.5 percent earned above $40,000 and accounted for 58.9 percent of our sample.

Table 8
Perpetrator's Salary*

Salary	Percentage
$20,000 and less	60.1
$20,001 to 30,000	18.9
$30,001 to 50,000	16.0
More than $50,000	5.0

* The frauds analyzed occured between the late 1960s and the early 1980s. Salary and data not adjusted for inflation.

Perpetrators' sex was not significantly cross-correlated to industrial type. One might expect that the incidence of fraud among females would be larger for certain company types because of traditionally higher percentages of women employed by some industries (i.e., financial institutions), but this was not the case. Perpetrators' sex was significantly cross-correlated with job level (p-value = .001) and amount defrauded (p-value = .005). Females frequently held clerical positions and defrauded smaller amounts. Our study showed that males perpetrated 51.7 percent of the frauds less than $40,000 (women, 48.3 percent). Males perpetrated 78.3 percent of the frauds over $100,000 and 92 percent of the frauds over $200,000. Only 11.6 percent of the women defrauded amounts greater than $100,000.

Perpetrators reported as having prior involvement in fraudulent activities were 20.2 percent. Our data contained a vast percentage of smaller frauds detected early, and it is probable that these cases included many first-time offenders. And as we will discuss later, many perpetrators are not prosecuted and, therefore, do not have criminal records. Without a prior record, it is doubtful that an individual would confess to any prior fraudulent involvement.

Audit directors reported that, in 38.1 percent of the cases, perpetrators were described as being among the company's best employees prior to the fraud detection. The defrauders were classified as "average" in 58.9 percent and as "worst" in only 3 percent of the cases. The communications/reports of the perpetrators, however, were reported by 64 percent of those interviewed as being "unreliable." Although this figure has the obvious benefit of hindsight, it is nonetheless meaningful. If we auditors meet employees that are considered among the company's best whose communications often prove unreliable, we should be aware that this factor combination was prevalent in our reported cases. Many audit directors said that defrauders *had* to be among the best employees in order to perpetrate and cover up the fraud while performing at least satisfactory work.

What do our findings suggest so far? Although an oversimplification, we could describe the average perpetrator in our sample as a young-to-middle-aged married male, a graduate from high school earning about $20,000 as a supervisor, one who has not been involved in prior fraudulent activities, and who is typically characterized as an above-average-to-outstanding employee. Keep in mind, however, that personal characteristics usually offer little value when attempting to distinguish fraud perpetrators from the average employee. In the context of company type, fraud amount and other demographic factors, however, certain characteristics seem to have a significant correlation to fraud. Knowledge of these areas should assist an auditor when identifying situations where fraud exposure is greater than what is normally acceptable. A later section addresses this aspect.

Action Against Perpetrators

Once a fraud is uncovered, a company must determine what action to take against the perpetrator. Table 9 shows that 51.2 percent of the reported cases resulted in prosecution. This percentage is probably due to the high cost of prosecuting, coupled with embarrassing publicity for companies and their management, the difficulty in obtaining court-admissable evidence, the low dollar amount of the reported cases, and the reluctance of public officials to prosecute cases when companies have recovered funds. We believe that the lack of prosecution probably encourages the perpetrators and diminishes fraud deterrence. In fact, it is possible that, because some companies are unwilling to prosecute, employees fail to see the severity of the act.

Table 9
Action Taken Against Perpetrator

Action	Percentage
No Action	1.5
Disciplined	.5
Transferred	.5
Terminated, not prosecuted	34.1
Terminated and prosecuted	51.2
Other	12.2

As Table 10 indicates, only a small percentage of the prosecuted cases resulted in an innocent verdict. Close inspection, however, reveals some very curious facts. Although 97.7 percent of the prosecutions resulted in guilty verdicts, only 31.4 percent of the prosecuted perpetrators were incarcerated. Of those, 52 percent were incarcerated two years or less. Twenty percent were incarcerated between two and five years.

Table 10
Verdict If Prosecuted

Verdict	Percentage
Not Guilty	2.3
Guilty – suspended	19.8
Guilty – probation	46.5
Guilty – incarcerated	31.4

Therefore, once a perpetrator is caught the probability of being prosecuted, found guilty, and incarcerated for more than two years is 7.7 percent. If we assume half of the frauds are detected – and this is a very conservative figure – the chance is four in 100 (3.8 percent) of being found and incarcerated for more than two years. In our sample, 48.8 percent of the cases were never prosecuted.

Table 11
Length of Incarceration

Years	Percentage
1 and less	28.0
1 to 2	24.0
2 to 3	8.0
3 to 5	16.0
More than 5	24.0

The action of the company, the verdict/sentence, and years incarcerated resulted in more meaningful cross-correlations. Industry type was not statistically correlated with action taken, verdict/sentence, or years incarcerated. No particular industry, therefore, appears to be more or less punitive on fraud perpetrators. Education level of the perpetrator also made no difference in the perpetrators' action taken, verdict, or sentence. An analysis of fraud amount revealed no significant correlation with the action taken (p-value = .252). The verdict/sentence when prosecuted, however, was significantly correlated. Of the cases over $200,000, 83.3 percent were found guilty and incarcerated – none of the perpetrators in this category were determined innocent or given suspended sentences. On the other hand, only 9.1 percent of the prosecuted cases involving less than $20,000 were incarcerated. So, of all those incarcerated, 61.6 percent of the defrauded amounts were over $100,000. The p-value significance for this correlation was .002.

Once the guilty judgment was passed, the length of time incarcerated was not correlated to the fraud amount. There appeared to be some trends in the data, although they were not statistically significant. For example, all the incarcerations over five years (see Table 11) were for frauds over $100,000, but not all frauds of this size were incarcerated that long. Forty-one percent of the perpetrators in this dollar category were incarcerated less than two years. All perpetrators who had defrauded less than $40,000 were incarcerated less than two years.

The data on salaries provided interesting results. Although neither the action taken against the perpetrator nor the verdict/sentence was significantly correlated with the perpetrator's salary, there were notable trends in the verdict/sentence data. Of the perpetrators incarcerated, 72 percent earned $20,000 and less per year; only 12 percent made more than $40,000 per year. Recall that the fraud amount and salary were significantly correlated and that persons earning higher salaries defrauded larger amounts.

Once sentenced and incarcerated, the perpetrators' salaries apparently influenced their length of imprisonment. Of those making $40,000 or less, 63.6 percent were jailed for less than three years. (We should note that the small number of perpetrators in our sample who were incarcerated limits the applicability of certain statistical tests because of a failure to meet some of the assumptions of the statistical models. This is at least part of the reason the trends just described were not statistically significant.)

The perpetrators' sex was significantly correlated to the action taken and the verdict/sentence given. A statistically significant higher percentage of female perpetrators was prosecuted; they were terminated and prosecuted 61.2 percent of the time versus 43.7 percent for males. Women were terminated but *not* prosecuted in 28.2 percent of the cases versus 38.7 percent for men.

The verdict/sentence for men and women was also statistically different (p-value = .025). Men were incarcerated more than women. The latter who were prosecuted were given suspended or probationary sentences in 79 percent of the cases, but only 9.5 percent of the male perpetrators were given suspended sentences. None of the women perpetrators in the study were found innocent. Once found guilty and sentenced, however, there was no significant difference between men and women in the number of years they were imprisoned, even though there existed very significant differences between the sexes in regard to the average dollar amounts defrauded.

Table 12
Perpetrator's Sex and Verdict/Sentence

	Verdict/Sentence (Percentage)			
Sex	Not Guilty	Guilty – Suspended	Guilty – Probation	Guilty – Incarcerated
Male	4.8	9.5	45.2	40.5
Female	0.0	30.2	48.8	20.9

In many cases a company can recover some of the defrauded funds from a bonding company or the perpetrator. In our study 63.4 percent of the companies did not recover funds from a bonding company, whereas 37 percent did. In 60 percent of the cases, companies were unable to recover any funds from the perpetrator. One-third of the reported companies could not recover funds from either the perpetrator or a bonding company.

The amount recovered from bonding companies was significantly correlated to the amount defrauded. Generally, as the dollar amount of the fraud increased, the amount recovered increased. The amount recovered from the perpetrator was also correlated with the amount of the fraud. The larger frauds recovered more total dollars but the larger the fraud category, the smaller the percentage of cases where some amount was recoverable from the perpetrator.

Motivation for Fraud

The internal audit directors were asked to classify the fraud's cause as being (1) a lack of internal control, (2) failure to enforce existing internal control, or (3) management's overriding of existing internal control. The first selection was cited as the primary cause of fraud in 50.3 percent of the cases. Failure to enforce controls drew 37.3 percent of the vote, whereas management's override of control settled for third with 12.4 percent. These results are somewhat contradictory when compared to the responses of audit directors who were asked to describe the fraud cause. When asked "What condition allowed the fraud to be perpetrated and to go undetected?" the majority responded with comments like:

- Lack of compliance with prescribed segregation of duties.
- Extreme trust in a key employee.
- Lack of management attention to detail.
- Too much delegation of duties.

The auditors frequently implied that controls had been established but were not adhered to or that detail was lacking. In a typical scenario, a manager identified an employee as a hard worker who accepted responsibility. Because the manager grew busier, more responsibility was delegated to this key employee. Subsequently, the manager failed to properly supervise and review the employee's work. This seemed appropriate because of the employee's performance and perceived honesty. Thus, the key employee was able to perpetrate a fraud even though controls had been established.

As an example of inadequate attention to detail, one audit director told of a fraud that was perpetrated by someone who was taking cash received and posting the funds as "deposits in transit." The home office reconciled the account monthly but failed to notice the detail – some of the deposits in transit were over a year old!

Both of these examples could be interpreted as a lack of internal control. Thus, some directors might have classified frauds as being caused by a lack of controls rather than failure to enforce existing controls. The low percentage of frauds reportedly caused by management's overriding controls is logical when given the majority of "smaller" frauds and the infrequency of collusion.

Fraud cause and perpetrators' sex were significantly correlated (p-value = .019). Table 13 indicates that cases of fraud perpetrated by women were caused more often by a lack of internal control than any other reason. Only 4.9 percent of the female perpetrators had overridden internal controls. This relates to the fact that women held clerical positions and perpetrated the smaller fraud amounts.

Table 13
Fraud Cases

Causes (percentage)

Sex	Lack of Internal Control	Failure to Enforce	Management Override
Male	49.5	32.4	18.0
Female	51.9	43.2	4.9

When asked how the fraud was detected, only 18 percent of those interviewed indicated an audit investigation. Most frauds – 32.8 percent – were detected through customer complaints or other employees, anonymous tips, etc. Regular operating-department reviews/procedures detected a mere 18.4 percent of the cases.

Only 25.7 percent of the internal audit departments responding to our questionnaire had a formally written policy regarding actions to be taken upon the detection of a possible fraud. In a majority of cases, the policy simply called for management to "contact legal counsel" or "notify security." Few, if any, outlined steps to protect the company and/or a perpetrator's rights or methods of gathering/securing evidence. Limited training regarding the legal rules associated with evidence or action to ensure the usability of audit evidence in a court case had transpired.

It was surprising to learn that 7.3 percent of the directors described management's support of fraud investigations as "indifferent, discouraging, or impeding." The term used by 62.6 percent of the directors was "enthusiastic support."

Actual and Perceived Importance of Factors

In the last section, the demographic factors of the frauds and perpetrators were explained, but now the frequencies of the actual and the perceived red flags are examined.

Explanation of Questionnaire – Perpetrators

Our questionnaire asked the participants to evaluate two sets of 25 factors dealing with the perpetrator and the company environment. We will examine the participant factors first and start with factor one.

1. **Unusually High Personal Debts**

		N/A		
	SD*	D	SwD	DKn	Swa	A	SA

a. The perpetrator(s) had unusually ( ) ( ) ( ) ( ) ( ) ( ) ( )
    high personal debts.

b. Generally speaking, knowledge
    that an employee had unusually
    high personal debts would in-
    crease my awareness of the pos-
    sibility of fraud by that employ- ( ) ( ) ( ) ( ) ( ) ( ) ( )
    ee.

c. This type of data on employees is: _____ readily available;
    _____ available; but difficult to obtain; _____ unavailable.

d. If this information were available, should the company maintain it
    on all key employees?
    _____ yes _____ no

e. If the information should not be maintained ("no" response to "d"),
    why not? (Check all that apply).
    _____ too costly.
    _____ negative impact on employee morale.
    _____ possibly illegal.
    _____ lack authority to collect data.
    _____ too confidential.
    _____ wouldn't be of any value.
    _____ other(s).

*SD = Strongly Disagree; D = Disagree; SwD = Somewhat Disagree; N/A, DKn = Not Applicable, Don't Know; SwA = Somewhat Agree; A = Agree; SA = Strongly Agree.

The questionnaire instructions tell the survey participant to answer question "a" in the context of a specific fraud that his or her company had experienced. Respondents marked their answers to the first 21 perpetrator-related questions on the seven-point scale. They either expressed some degree of agreement that the factor existed in their specific fraud, some degree of disagreement, that they either didn't know the answer, or that it wasn't applicable in their circumstances. The last four perpetrator-related questions were changed to include either yes, no, or don't-know answers for logic/clarity.

Questions "b" through "e" in the perpetrator-related section did not relate to a specific fraud. Participants were asked to assess the value of the factor in the overall detection of fraud. What purpose did this serve? We wanted their opinions about whether factor information would increase awareness of the possibility of fraud. Their responses were measured on the same seven-point scale used in question "a."

The third question dealt with the perception of the availability of information regarding the factor. The participants had three choices: readily available, available but difficult to obtain, and unavailable. The fourth question asked if respondents felt the company should keep records of information on all key employees. Those who felt the information should not be maintained were then asked in question "e" to specify their reasons. We offered six choices plus allowed for flexibility of explanations via their expressions/answers.

A distinguishing characteristic of many fraud perpetrators is that, rather than stash the cash, they consume the embezzled funds. This allows them to enjoy a lifestyle beyond their reach with their present salary . Because we felt it important to know what the perpetrators had done with their ill-gotten gains, we asked the question: To your knowledge, did the perpetrator use the embezzled resources to obtain any of the following:

	Yes	No	Don't Know
a. Expensive automobiles?	___	___	___
b. Extravagant vacations?	___	___	___
c. Extravagant wardrobe?	___	___	___
d. New or remodeled house?	___	___	___
e. Recreational property (boat, cabin, motor home)?	___	___	___
f. Support of extramarital relationships?	___	___	___
g. Other (please describe)?	___	___	___

Questionnaire Results

In these results, the answers to "a" are referred to as facts (i.e., fact mean, fact rank). The answers to question "b" are referred to as perceptions (i.e., perception mean, perception rank).

Table 14
Perpetrator Characteristics: Ranking by Fact Mean*

Perpetrator Characteristics	Fact Mean	Fact Rank	Perception Rank
Living Beyond Means	4.397	1	2
Overwhelming Desire for Personal Gain	4.051	2	14
High Personal Debt	3.938	3	4
Close Association with Customers	3.821	4	15
Believed Pay Not Commensurate	3.811	5	16
Wheeler Dealer	3.791	6	11
Challenge to Beat the System	3.489	7	5
Excessive Gambling Habits	3.312	8	1
Undue Family/Peer Pressure	3.214	9	24
No Recognition for Job Performance	3.156	10	21
Close Association with Suppliers	3.130	11	6
Feeling of Job Dissatisfaction	3.085	12	19
Poor Credit Rating	3.024	13	12
Alcohol Problems	2.810	14	17
Severe Personal Financial Loss	2.755	15	8
Lacked Personal Stability	2.734	16	18
Rationalizing Poor Performance	2.726	17	22
Investments	2.724	18	13
Drug Problems	2.634	19	9
Felt Job in Jeopardy	2.136	20	20
Continually Threatening to Quit	1.856	21	25

	Including Don't Know			Not Including Don't Know	
	Yes	No	Don't Know	Yes	No
Unreliable Communications	42.6%	23.9%	33.5%	64.0%	36.0%
No Time off Longer Than 2-3 Days	16.3%	58.2%	25.5%	21.9%	78.1%
Criminal Record	10.4%	64.8%	24.8%	13.9%	86.1%
Defendant in Civil Suit	4.7%	29.9%	65.4%	13.7%	86.3%

*Only 21 items are ranked because only 21 of the 25 questions were answered on the seven-point scale. The other four were answered on a yes-no-don't-know basis.

Table 14 shows the ranking of the 25 perpetrator characteristics by using the fact mean (the answer to question "a") as the ranking basis. Only 21 of the 25 factors are ranked because means, or "average" responses, could only be calculated for those answers on the seven-point scale. The means were determined by scratching out the don't-know/not-applicable responses and assigning one point to the strongly-disagree answers. Moving right on the scale, each item was incremented by one. The strongly-agree value, therefore, was assigned a value of six. Table 14 shows the factor, the fact mean, the ranking of the factors based upon the mean values, and the perception (question "b" answer) ranking.

Table 15
Perpetrator Characteristics: Ranking by
Perception Mean

Perpetrator Characteristics	Perception Mean	Rank	Fact Rank*
Excessive Gambling Habits	5.007	1	8
Living Beyond Means	4.973		
Criminal Record	4.924	3	NR
High Personal Debt	4.730	4	3
Challenge to Beat the System	4.696	5	7
Close Association with Suppliers	4.636	6	11
Unreliable Communications	4.614	7	NR
Severe Personal Financial Loss	4.608	8	15
Drug Problems	4.597	9	19
No Time off Longer Than 2-3 Days	4.497	10	NR
Wheeler Dealer	4.380	11	6
Poor Credit Rating	4.116	12	13
Extensive Involvement in Speculative Investments	4.094	13	18
Overwhelming Desire for Personal Gain	4.031	14	2
Close Association with Customers	3.935	15	4
Believed Pay Not Commensurate	3.922	16	5
Alcohol Problems	3.913	17	14
Lacked Personal Stability	3.904	18	16
Feeling of Job Dissatisfaction	3.794	19	12
Felt Job in Jeopardy	3.560	20	20
No Recognition for Job Performance	3.550	21	10
Rationalizing Poor Performance	3.375	22	17
Defendant in Civil Suit	3.355	23	NR
Undue Family/Peer Pressure	3.298	24	9
Continually Threatening to Quit	3.239	25	21

*The four items not ranked, due to a yes-no answer rather than a seven-point scale answer, are indicated in this column by an NR.

The 25 perpetrator characteristics and their rankings by using the perception mean as the basis are shown in Table 15. The perception means were calculated in the same manner as the fact means. All 25 items are ranked, since the seven-point scale was used for every question. Also shown in Table 15 are the perception means and the fact rank. The four characteristics without a fact mean rank were indicated by NR in the appropriate column.

The midpoint of our scale is 3.5. Based upon these criteria, we see in Table 14 that only the first six of the 21 items have means over 3.5 with the seventh very close at 3.489. Examining the yes/no answers shows that only the first item – "unreliable communications" – was present in more than 50 percent of the cases where the participant knew whether the factor was present or not. On the average, then, we could conclude that only six (possibly 8) of the 25 items were a factor in the average fraud.

On the other hand, using the same 3.5 cutoff, the participants agreed that all but the last four items listed in Table 15 were considered important predictors of fraudulent activity.

Tables 14 and 15 can also be used to compare the fact and the perception rankings. Gambling is the most important perception factor (5.007 mean) yet was only rated eighth (of 21) based on actual fraud facts. Other interesting differences include:

Factor	Perception Mean	Rank (1-25)	Fact Rank (1-21)	Mean
Believed pay not commensurate	3.922	16	5	3.811
Close association with customers	3.935	15	4	3.821
Drug problems	4.597	9	19	2.634
Feeling job dissatisfaction	3.794	19	12	3.085
No recognition for job performance	3.550	21	10	3.156
Overwhelming desire for personal gain	4.031	14	2	4.051
Severe personal financial losses	4.608	8	15	2.755
Undue family/peer pressure	3.298	24	9	3.214

"Continually threatening to quit" was ranked rock-bottom in the rankings; both means fall below the 3.5 cutoff. "Criminal record" had a perception rank of third, but participants indicated it was a consideration in only 13.9 percent of the cases where they knew whether it was a factor. "No time off longer than 2-3 days" had a perpetrator rank of tenth but came into play in only 21.9 percent of the cases where it was known whether the factor existed.

Table 16 shows the 25 factors (listed in the same order as Table 14) and summarizes the participants' answers to questions "c" through "e." The first three columns to the right of the factors summarize the participants' beliefs regarding the availability of

Table 16
Perpetrator Characteristics: Availability of Information

| | | Availability | | | Why Would Not Collect | | | | | | |
Fact Rank	Factor	Perception Rank	Readily Avail.	Avail.	Unavail.	Would Not Collect	Too Costly	Neg. Impact	Too Confidential	No Value	Illegal	Lack Authority
1	Living Beyond Means	2	7.3%	51.3%	41.4%	66.9%	50.0%	59.6%	51.0%	9.6%	57.5%	54.3%
2	Overwhelming Desire for Personal Gain	14	6.0	28.2	65.8	73.6	26.3	25.0	20.0	53.8	16.3	17.5
3	High Personal Debt	4	13.8	39.5	46.7	66.2	50.0	62.8	58.5	5.3	74.5	52.1
4	Close Association with Customers	15	27.7	46.6	25.7	50.4	38.1	23.8	11.1	55.6	17.5	14.3
5	Believed Pay Not Commensurate	16	17.7	42.2	40.1	60.9	22.4	25.0	18.4	60.5	11.8	15.8
6	Wheeler Dealer	11	20.1	40.9	38.9	67.6	34.1	22.7	18.2	39.8	29.6	28.4
7	Challenge to Beat the System	5	4.1	29.1	66.6	49.2	23.6	20.0	20.0	41.8	20.0	29.1
8	Excessive Gambling Habits	1	0.0	34.7	65.3	59.7	50.0	43.2	47.3	6.8	63.5	60.8
9	Undue Family/Peer Pressure	24	0.7	18.7	80.6	89.3	28.4	32.4	34.3	39.2	33.3	33.3
10	No Recognition for Job Performance	21	16.6	47.0	36.4	54.5	27.9	27.9	22.0	66.2	14.7	16.2
11	Close Association with Suppliers	6	19.6	54.7	25.7	34.8	42.2	22.2	11.1	40.0	24.44	17.8
12	Feeling of Job Dissatisfaction	19	20.4	49.3	30.3	50.0	25.0	28.1	21.9	57.8	21.9	17.2
13	Poor Credit Rating	12	41.4	42.2	16.4	61.6	48.3	46.1	50.6	16.9	57.3	39.3
14	Alcohol Problems	17	12.2	45.9	41.9	65.9	33.7	42.2	22.2	11.1	40.0	24.4
15	Severe Personal Financial Loss	8	1.3	33.1	65.6	68.0	44.3	60.2	58.0	6.8	64.8	56.8
16	Lacked Personal Stability	18	52.7	35.3	12.0	32.7	31.9	25.5	21.3	51.1	34.0	27.7
17	Rationalizing Poor Performance	22	42.3	33.5	24.2	45.9	20.7	20.7	12.1	70.7	13.8	10.3
18	Extensive Involvement in Speculative Investments	13	2.0	24.8	73.2	74.0	50.0	46.8	59.6	14.9	57.5	56.4
19	Drug Problems	9	2.7	40.1	57.2	51.1	44.8	43.3	62.7	7.5	58.2	50.8
20	Felt Job in Jeopardy	20	18.0	30.0	52.0	62.9	20.6	32.8	16.4	60.27	17.8	21.9
21	Continually Threatening to Quit	25	39.2	37.9	22.9	47.2	23.1	18.5	15.4	67.7	18.5	13.9
NR	Unreliable Communications	7	38.0	46.7	15.3	24.6	43.8	12.5	3.1	53.1	6.3	12.5
NR	No Time off Longer Than 2-3 Days	10	88.7	9.3	2.0	9.4	33.3	16.7	8.3	66.7	0.0	0.0
NR	Criminal Record	3	43.9	50.7	5.4	12.0	25.0	12.5	33.3	8.3	83.3	41.7
NR	Defendant in Criminal Suit	23	22.1	55.8	22.1	71.4	31.6	25.5	27.6	52.0	41.8	25.5

factor information. As the table reveals, in only two instances did the majority believe information on that factor was readily available. Less than 10 percent of the respondents thought the information was readily available for eight of the factors, but more than 50 percent disagreed and thought information was unavailable.

Question "d" asked if respondents would collect data if it were available. For 17 of the 25 factors, more than 50 percent said they *would not.*The reasons for their decision are shown in the six right-hand columns in Table 16. Many respondents indicated more than one reason, hence percentages do not add up to 100 percent.

What follows is a list of the more important reasons why respondents were not interested in gathering data:

	Too Costly	Neg. Impact	Too Conf.	No Value	Il-Legal	Lack of Authority
More than 50% wouldn't gather	4	3	7	12	9	6
Most frequently mentioned reason	1	1	2	15	6	0

This summary concludes that, for 12 of the 25 factors, more than 50 percent of the respondents would not collect information because they felt it had no value. All six reasons were listed by the majority for three or more of the factors. All but "lack of authority" was the most frequently listed reason for not collecting the data on one or more of the factors.

Table 16 also reveals that, when more than 50 percent of the respondents felt the item had no value, the other percentages were usually smaller than 50 percent. An example of this is "believed pay not commensurate." Over 60 percent felt information concerning this factor would be of no value. When the "no value" did not carry the lead, several other reasons emerged such as "living beyond means." Only 9.6 percent felt it would be of no value, but 50 percent of the respondents would not collect the information for each of the other five reasons.

The data show that, of the seven more important factors, all but 24.6 percent of the respondents would only be willing to collect information about one factor – "unreliable communications." Ironically, 53.1 percent of those unwilling to collect data claimed it had no value. From this we can conclude that internal auditors do not realize the importance of gathering the precise information that is most likely to help them evaluate whether a person is likely to commit a fraud!

The major reasons for not gathering information concerning the seven more important factors are shown below:

Fact Rank	Factor	Percep. Rank	Would Not Collect	Too Costly	Neg. Impact	Too Confi-dential	No Value	Il-legal	Lack of Auth-ority
1	Living Beyond means	2	66.9%	50.0%	59.6%	51.0%	9.6%	57.5%	54.3%
2	Overwhelming Desire for Personal Gain	14	73.6	26.3	25.0	20.0	53.8	16.3	17.5
3	High Personal Debt	4	66.2	50.0	62.8	58.5	5.3	74.5	52.1
4	Close Association with Customers	15	50.4	38.1	23.8	11.1	55.6	17.5	14.3
5	Believed Pay Not Commensurate	16	60.9	27.4	25.0	18.4	60.5	11.8	15.8
6	Wheeler Dealer	11	67.6	34.1	22.7	18.2	39.8	29.6	28.4
NR	Unreliable Communications	7	24.6	43.8	12.5	3.1	53.1	6.3	12.5

Of the seven reasons, only "wheeler dealer" does not follow the established pattern we've discovered. The reasons why information for this category would not be gathered are evenly distributed over the six categories. Thus, we can conclude that the majority of respondents feel that these important factors are either (1) viewed as having no value, (2) are too costly and too confidential to gather, (3) are illegal, (4) are not gathered because of a perceived negative impact, and/or (5) that internal auditors lack authority to gather them.

Table 17
Perpetrator Characteristics: Why Fraud Was Committed

Personal Characteristic Factors	Total	Response Percentage
Perpetrator Needed the Money or Desired Personal Gain	43	17.6
Perpetrator Was Living Beyond Means	35	14.4
Perpetrator Was in Debt	35	14.4
The Temptation Was Too Great	34	13.9
Greed	31	12.7
Vice (Gambling, Drugs, Alcohol)	23	9.4
Perpetrator Had Contempt for Company or Had Abnormally Low Pay	16	6.6
Perpetrator Wanted to Lead a Wild Life	9	3.7
Family Problems	7	2.9
Emotional (Mental Illness)	5	2.0
Perpetrator Was the Dishonest Type	3	1.2
Perpetrator Wanted to Blackmail the Company	2	.8
Perpetrator Needed a "Loan"	1	.4
	244[1]	100%

[1]This number exceeds the 212-questionnaire return because some people gave more than one answer.

In the preliminary demographics section of the questionnaire, we asked the following question: "In your opinion, why did the perpetrator commit the fraud?" This was posed before any of the perpetrator or company characteristics were mentioned. Our initial intent was for the respondents to tell us in their own words and before being biased by our questions what they believed caused the perpetrator to commit the fraud. Table 17 lists their responses and shows how many times the reasons were mentioned along with the percentage each answer was given. The more common responses dealt with indebtedness, a particular lifestyle, or the desire to get "rich."

Table 18
Perpetrator Characteristics: Uses of Fraudulently Obtained Funds

Funds were used by the perpetrators for the following items:

Expensive Automobiles	29.8%
New/Remodeled Home	29.3%
Support Extramarital Relationships	28.7%
Extravagant Wardrobe	24.7%
Recreational Property	24.6%
Extravagant Vacations	21.8%

After the perpetrator questions had been completed, we asked respondents to tell us what goods or services had been purchased by the perpetrators with their illegal funds. Table 18 shows the results of this question with the answers evenly distributed among six categories.

Explanation of Questionnaire – Organizational Environment

The third major section of the questionnaire covered the "organizational environment" in which the perpetrator worked. Survey participants were asked to respond to 25 questions which used the same seven-point-scale format. For example, let's review "competent personnel":

				N/A			
1. Competent Personnel	SD	D	SwD	DKn	SwA	A	SA
a. The department lacked competent personnel.	( )	( )	( )	( )	( )	( )	( )
b. Generally incompetent personnel makes it easier for fraud to be perpetrated.	( )	( )	( )	( )	( )	( )	( )
c. Comments _____							

After survey participants responded to the 25 factors, they were asked to indicate management's reaction to the fraud investigation as being "enthusiastically supportive, generally supportive, indifferent, discouraged the investigation, or impeded the investigation."

Questionnaire Results

Tables 19 and 20 are similar to tables 14 and 15 except that organizational environment factors are listed rather than perpetrator characteristics. In Table 14, the 25 factors are shown in fact rank order along with the fact mean and the perception rank. In Table 15, the 25 factors are shown in perception-rank order with the perception mean and the fact rank.

Table 19
Organizational Environment: Fact Ranking

Organizational Environment Characteristics	Fact Mean	Fact Rank	Perception Rank
Too Much Trust in Key Employees	4.677	1	9
Lack Proper Procedures for Authorizations	4.480	2	1
Lack Personal Investment Income Disclosure	4.478	3	25
No Separation of Transaction Authorization from Custody	4.299	4	3
No Independent Checks on Performance	4.292	5	7
Lack Adequate Attention to Detail	4.221	6	10
No Separation of Asset Custody from Accounting	4.111	7	2
No Separation of Accounting Duties	3.982	8	4
Lack of Clear Lines of Authority	3.933	9	6
Department Not Frequently Reviewed	3.645	10	14
No Conflict-of-Interest Statement	3.590	11	23
Inadequate Documents and Records	3.565	12	5
Background Not Adequately Checked	3.323	13	13
Incompetent Personnel	3.256	14	8
Department Operates on Crisis Basis	3.157	15	15
Failed to Discipline Violators of Policy	2.959	16	12
Lack Explicit Uniform Personnel Policies	2.776	17	19
Inadequate Physical Security	2.763	18	11
Department Inadequately Staffed	2.635	19	18
Department Budget Not Reviewed, Justified	2.567	20	16
Pay Not Commensurate with Responsibility	2.508	21	20
Unrealistic Productivity Expectations	2.454	22	24
Not Informed About Company Disciplinary Rules	2.333	23	21
Not Operating Under a Budget	2.308	24	17
No Record of Disciplinary Actions	2.221	25	22

Table 20
Organizational Environment: Perception Ranking

Organizational Environment Characteristics	Perception Mean	Perception Rank	Fact Rank
Lack Proper Procedures for Authorizations	5.383	1	2
No Separation of Asset Custody from Accounting	5.357	2	7
No Separation of Transaction Authorization from Custody	5.269	3	4
No Separation of Accounting Duties	5.245	4	8
Inadequate Documents and Records	5.218	5	12
Lack of Clear Lines of Authority	4.973	6	9
No Independent Checks on Performance	4.964	7	5
Incompetent Personnel	4.959	8	14
Too Much Trust in Key Employees	4.884	9	1
Lack Adequate Attention to Detail	4.807	10	6
Inadequate Physical Security	4.743	11	18
Failed to Discipline Violators of Policy	4.725	12	16
Background Not Adequately Checked	4.641	13	13
Department Not Frequently Reviewed	4.593	14	10
Department Operates on a Crisis Basis	4.540	15	15
Department Budget Not Reviewed, Justified	4.474	16	20
Not Operating Under a Budget	4.357	17	24
Department Inadequately Staffed	4.347	18	19
Lack Explicit Uniform Personnel Policies	4.338	19	17
Pay Not Commensurate with Responsibility	3.992	20	21
Not Informed About Company Disciplinary Rules	3.977	21	23
No Record of Disciplining Actions	3.924	22	25
No Conflict-of-Interest Statement	3.881	23	11
Unrealistic Productivity Expectations	3.838	24	22
Lack Personal Investment Income Disclosure	3.274	25	3

Using a mean value of 3.5 once again as the cutoff between agreement and disagreement, we find that 12 of the 25 items on Table 19 had a fact mean greater than 3.5 and that all but one had a perception mean greater than 3.5. The one with the mean less than 3.5 – "lack of personal investment-income disclosure" – was close to the 3.5 mean with a 3.274.

A comparison of fact and perception means reveals some interesting results. The third important organizational environment characteristic – according to the fact means, the "lack-of-disclosure" factor – ranked dead last in the perception rankings. The "no-conflict-of-interest statement," ranked 11th according to fact means, was 23rd in the perception rankings. None of the other rankings differed by more than seven points on the 25-point-scale ranking. A logical conclusion is that internal auditors don't understand the importance of a personal investment-income disclosure and a conflict-of-interest statement. It is possible that the use of these two documents could help deter fraud.

Cross-Correlations Between Fraud Variables

In the last section, actual frequencies of the fraud factors were analyzed and their rankings are interesting when examining fraud in general. However, there may be some factors that are good predictors of certain types of frauds (e.g., large ones) but not others (e.g., small ones). Examples of these types of factors might be that receiving inadequate pay is a motivating factor for small but not for large frauds, that having extramarital relations might be a red flag for frauds perpetrated by men but not by women, that only perpetrators with high educational levels perpetrate large-dollar frauds, or that close association with suppliers might motivate frauds in some industries but not in others. In order to analyze these kinds of correlations, we cross-tabulated some of the fraud variables with all others. Specifically, the five variables used for the cross-correlators were:

1. Amount of the fraud vs. all other perpetrator and company factors.
2. Sex of perpetrator vs. all other perpetrator and company factors.
3. Education level of perpetrator vs. all other perpetrator and company factors.
4. Salary of perpetrator vs. all other perpetrator and company factors.
5. Type of company against which fraud was perpetrated vs. all other perpetrator and company factors.

These types of cross-tabulations were chosen because they were considered logical. "Amount of fraud" was selected because it was felt that those factors that motivated small frauds might be very different from those that motivated large frauds. "Sex of perpetrator" was chosen because men and women often react differently to environmental and personal pressures. Therefore, what motivates a female to perpetrate a fraud may seem insignificant to males and vice versa. "Education level" was listed because perpetrators with college degrees or advanced training might be motivated by intellectual challenges or work frustrations, while employees with less education might react more dramatically to financial pressures. "Salary of perpetrator" was selected because perpetrators with higher incomes might not commit smaller frauds, while those with lower salaries might be inclined to commit fraud for any amount. Finally, "type of company" was chosen because, just as environments differ in various industries, fraud motivations might differ. For example, bank tellers might commit fraud because of the inability to cope with the daily temptation of handling cash, while employees in a manufacturing firm might be motivated by other pressures and opportunities. Let's examine the cross-correlations separately.

Fraud Amount vs. Perpetrator Factors

The significance of the cross-correlations were measured by using chi-square analysis. Table 21 shows the significance levels (chi-square statistics) for each of the 31 red flags including the 31 originals plus the six ways perpetrators spend money.

The chi-square statistics of the factors are ranked from most to least significant. In examining "size of fraud," the 212 cases were classified into six categories – under \$20,000, \$20,000 - \$40,000, \$40,000 - \$60,000, \$60,000 - \$100,000, \$100,000 - \$200,000, and more than \$200,000.

Significance levels were .000 for "using fraud proceeds to purchase a new home or remodel an existing home," "using fraud proceeds to take extravagant vacations," and "using fraud proceeds to purchase expensive automobiles." In many cases, perpetrators of large frauds used their funds to upgrade houses, take extravagant vacations, and buy expensive automobiles, while perpetrators of small frauds did not. This does not mean, however, that every perpetrator of a large or small fraud used his or her proceeds in this manner. Rather, it means that perpetrators of large frauds were perhaps more likely to spend their monies in these areas than were perpetrators of small frauds. As Table 21 indicates, the same result rings true in regard to those perpetrators who used their proceeds to purchase extravagant wardrobes, buy recreation property, and support extramarital relationships.

The next significant factor, "intellectually challenged to beat the system," is noteworthy because perpetrators motivated by such risks tend to be very good, creative employees. As the results show, they use their creativity to perpetrate large frauds. According to the data, those who are intellectually challenged are far more likely to perpetrate a large fraud instead of a small one. Likewise, small-fraud perpetrators are seldom motivated by intellectual challenges. This result is . . . *frightening!* The creative perpetrators are successfully committing the larger and more awesome frauds, while the smaller frauds with unsophisticated concealment methods are the ones being detected.

Table 21
Significance of Amount of Fraud
and Perpetrator Factors

Factor	P-Value
New/Remodeled Home	.000*
Extravagant Vacations	.000*
Expensive Automobiles	.000*
Extravagant Wardrobe	.003*
Recreation Property	.023*
Supported Extramarital Relationships	.026*
Challenged to Beat System	.036*
Felt Pay Not Commensurate with Responsibility	.038*
Extensive Involvement in Speculative Investments	.043*
Close Association with Suppliers	.072
Lacked Personal Stability	.117
Undue Family/Peer Pressure	.139
Excessive Gambling Habits	.157
No Time off Longer Than 2-3 Days	.159
Close Association with Customers	.164
Believed Job in Jeopardy	.183
High Personal Debt	.230
Provided Unreliable Communications	.252
Rationalized Poor Performance	.253
Severe Personal Financial Loss	.290
Continually Threatening to Quit	.293
Alcohol Problems	.306
A Wheeler Dealer	.307
Poor Credit Rating	.354
Living Beyond Means	.401
Drug Problems	.484
A Civil-Suit Defendant	.507
Overwhelming Desire for Personal Gain	.602
Lack Recognition of Job Performance	.676
A Criminal Record	.818
Feeling of Job Dissatisfaction	.829

* = Significant at .05 level.

A perception that "pay is not commensurate with responsibility" appears to be a motivating factor for both very small and the very large frauds but not for those of medium size. While we are unsure of the reasons, perhaps perpetrators of small frauds just take as much as they feel they deserve, while perpetrators of large frauds have the underlying motive to get even with their companies. This perception is supported by the details of one small fraud where the perpetrator was making $15,000 a year but thought a 10 percent pay hike was in order. He proceeded to steal exactly $125 a month for the next year.

The final significant factor, "extensive involvement in speculative investments," appears to motivate the large frauds but not the small ones. As evidence, 54 percent of frauds over $100,000 were used to support speculative investments, while 69 percent of those under $60,000 were not.

Fraud Amount vs. Company Factors

Table 22 shows there are seven company factors where the size of the fraud seems to make a difference. Three of these — "separating the custody of assets from the accounting for those assets," "separating duties within the accounting function," and "separating the authorization of transactions from the recording of those transactions" — are clearly elements of a good internal

Table 22
Significance of Amount of Fraud vs. Company Factors

Factor	P-Value
Separation of Custody of Assets from Accounting	.001[*]
Separation of Accounting Function Duties	.004[*]
Unrealistic Productivity Expectations	.005[*]
Department Operated on "Crisis-Management" Basis	.013[*]
Competent Personnel	.017[*]
Excessive Trust in Key Employee	.019[*]
Separation of Authorization and Recording of Transactions	.026[*]
Clearly Defined Personnel Policies	.097
Attention to Detail	.158
Records of Discipline	.182
Clear Lines of Authority	.220
Pay Not Commensurate with Responsibility	.230
Failure to Discipline Policy Violators	.238
Conflict-of-Interest Statement Not Required	.240
Inadequate Physical Security	.276
Budget Review Lacking	.301
Disclosure of Personal Investments	.424
Adequate Documents and Records	.455
Inadequate Background Check Before Employment	.464
Independent Checks on Performance	.462
Department Inadequately Staffed	.612
Proper Procedures for Authorization	.624
Department Lacked Budgeted Operation	.734
Not Informed of Company Policy	.775
Department Not Frequently Reviewed	.868

[*] = Significant at .05 level.

control system. In each case, weakness in these control areas allowed for larger rather than smaller frauds. We believe this occurs because failure to enforce such controls makes fraud easier to cover up and harder to detect. If you believe that there is no such thing as a small fraud – only large ones given insufficient time to grow – then these control weaknesses simply give frauds ample opportunity to mature. Generally, people who use their access to control systems are unlikely to have been perpetrators before. And if they become trust violators through perceived opportunities, they may want to steal enough to make the dishonest act be worthwhile.

As with the previous three factors, having incompetent personnel tends to inspire larger rather than smaller frauds. Incompetent personnel make it easier to rely on the perpetrator. In that situation, perpetrators can more easily override existing controls and conceal their acts.

The final environmental factors – "imposing unrealistic productivity expectations," "operating on a crisis basis," and "placing excessive trust in key employees" – all lead to potentially larger frauds. In fact, particicipants usually answered "very strongly disagree" when asked if these factors allow small frauds but "very strongly agree" when commenting about large frauds.

Sex vs. Perpetrator Factors

Table 23 shows sex of perpetrator is a discriminator in only three of the 31 perpetrator factors. Of these, being a "wheeler dealer" is most significant and was more common among men than women. There could be two reasons for this finding: either women are not as likely to be wheeler-dealers, or those who are do not commit fraud.

The second factor, "close association with suppliers," was usually associated more with men rather than with women. Once again, this is probably because women generally do not have close association with suppliers or because those who do are not motivated to commit fraud.

As was the case with the other two sex-related factors, "a feeling of job dissatisfaction" tends to motivate men to commit fraud more so than women. From the data, it is impossible to tell whether women are pleased with their jobs or whether those who are dissatisfied don't commit fraud. One possible explanation is that women can handle frustration and dissatisfaction better than men. As a result, men may use dissatisfaction as a rationalization, while women do not.

Although it only has a significance level of .089, we believe "lack of personal stability" deserves discussion. Unstable women tend to commit fraud more often than do thier male counterparts. With this in mind, it may be important to closely monitor such disruptions as divorce, frequent moves, and other personal problems faced by women employees.

Table 23
Significance of Perpetrator's Sex
and Perpetrator Factors

Factor	P-Value
A Wheeler Dealer	.000*
Close Association With Suppliers	.0001*
Feeling of Job Dissatisfaction	.010*
Extensive Involvement in Speculative Investments	.081
Lacked Personal Stability	.089
Supported Extramarital Relationships	.099
Recreation Property	.118
A Criminal Record	.120
Lack of Recognition of Job Performance	.154
Challenged to Beat the System	.155
Rationalized Poor Performance	.205
Excessive Gambling Habits	.206
Extravagant Vacations	.217
Poor Credit Rating	.221
Believed Job in Jeopardy	.264
Living Beyond Means	.269
Severe Personal Financial Loss	.308
Extravagant Wardrobe	.309
No Time off Longer than 2-3 Days	.369
Overwhelming Desire for Personal Gain	.527
New/Remodeled Home	.566
Close Association with Customers	.611
Drug Problems	.618
Felt Pay Not Commensurate with Responsibility	.650
Continually Threatening to Quit	.730
Alcohol Problems	.752
Undue Family/Peer Pressure	.786
Expensive Automobiles	.892
High Personal Debt	.970
Provided Unreliable Communications	.978
A Civil-Suit Defendant	1.000

* = Significant at .05 level.

Sex vs. Company Factors

There is only one company factor, according to Table 24, where sex seems to make a difference. It appears that "operating on a crisis basis" is a factor more closely associated with men committing fraud than with women. As an example, our interview with one major company confirmed that most frauds are not committed in the "normal" environment but when crash projects or crisis conditions exist. It is at these times that traditional controls fall by the wayside and when men take advantage of such conditions to perpetrate fraud. This result suggests that women are more methodical in their frauds, while men are more impulsive. Also, because a higher percentage of men are in supervisory positions, "crash" projects allow them to override controls easier than women who are mainly in clerical positions.

Table 24
Significance of Perpetrator's Sex and Company Factors

Factor	P-Value
Department Operated on "Crisis Management" Basis	.039*
Adequate Documents and Records	.097
Department Inadequately Staffed	.124
Competent Personnel	.1741
Budget Review Lacking	.286
Conflict-of-Interest Statement Not Required	.298
Clearly Defined Personnel Policies	.290
Failure to Discipline Policy Violators	.346
Inadequate Background Check Before Employment	.368
Department Lacked Budgeted Operations	.521
Not Informed of Company Policy	.533
Unrealistic Productivity Expectations	.579
Independent Checks on Performance	.597
Separation of Accounting Function Duties	.631
Proper Procedures for Authorization	.632
Separation of Authorization and Recording of Transaction	.649
Pay Not Commensurate with Responsibility	.702
Excessive Trust in Key Employee	.814
Disclosure of Personal Investments	.887
Department Not Frequently Reviewed	.902
Inadequate Physical Security	.928
Attention to Detail	.966
Records of Discipline	.988
Separation of Custody from Accounting	1.000
Clear Lines of Authority	1.000

* = Significant at .05 level.

47

In general, there really aren't many red flags where sex makes a significant difference. This statement suggests that, with the exception of the few situations mentioned above, one cannot differentiate fraud detection and prevention efforts between men and women – both are seemingly affected by the same pressures and opportunities.

Education vs. Perpetrator Factors

To evaluate education level, fraud perpetrators were classified into three groups – high school graduate or less, some college

Table 25
Significance of Education Level and Perpetrator Factors

Factor	P-Value
A Wheeler Dealer	.000*
Close Association with Suppliers	.000*
Extravagant Vacations	.0001*
Recreation Property	.018*
Extravagant Wardrobe	.018*
Expensive Automobiles	.023*
Overwhelming Desire for Personal Gain	.023*
Supported Extramarital Relationships	.076*
Lack of Recognition of Job Performance	.122
Challenged to Beat System	.125
Extensive Involvement in Speculative Investments	.131
Drug Problems	.135
Severe Personal Financial Loss	.154
Undue Family/Peer Pressure	.185
Poor Credit Rating	.232
New/Remodeled Home	.2811
Feeling of Job Dissatisfaction	.282
A Civil-Suit Defendant	.337
A Criminal Record	.353
Believed Job in Jeopardy	.356
Rationalized Poor Performance	.443
Close Association with Customers	.478
Continually Threatening to Quit	.490
Excessive Gambling Habits	.612
Provided Unreliable Communications	.641
High Personal Debt	.671
Living Beyond Means	.757
Alcohol Problems	.879
Felt Pay Not Commensurate with Responsibility	.8801
Lacked Personal Stability	.938
No Time off Longer Than 2-3 Days	.948

* = Significant at .05 level.

but not graduated, and college graduate or more. As Table 25 shows, there are seven perpetrator factors where educational level is significant. In four factors, higher education seems to be associated with more fraud. Specifically, the more educated a person, the more likely is he or she to be a wheeler-dealer who commits fraud. Likewise, the more educated one is, the more likely is he or she will use supplier associations to perpetrate fraud. And the more education people have, the greater the chance that their desire for personal gain will motivate them to commit fraud.

The other three significant factors and "supporting extramarital relationships" (significance of .076) are all ways that perpetrators use their illegally obtained funds. It is interesting to note that all four – "taking extravagant vacations," "purchasing recreation property," "buying expensive automobiles," and "supporting extramarital relationships" – appear to motivate those who started but didn't finish college. And perpetrators who didn't attend or complete college appear to commit fraud because of these extravagant habits. This may suggest that perpetrators in this educational category are more likely to take shortcuts in order to achieve the same desired end as college graduates. Because they can't legally afford these habits, they take another route – fraud.

Education vs. Company Factors

Table 26 shows there are only three company factors where educational level appears to make a significant difference. The first – "a department that lacks competent personnel" – is significant because a higher educated employee working with "incompetents" tends to commit more fraud than one working with employees of the same or greater caliber. Why? The perceived increased opportunity makes it easier to take advantage of the situation.

Unrealistic productivity expectations motivates employees with college educations to commit fraud, although it is not as significant a factor for those with only a high school education. College graduates expected to perform but who fail become frustrated and the dilemma often leads to fraud. Perhaps we should reevaluate our expectations of college graduates! While they may meet our expectations in most cases, fraud can be the end result of those situations when they don't.

The final company factor where education level appears to play a major role is the mandatory conflict-of-interest statement or code of ethics. Such a statement seems to deter those employees with limited education but has minimal deterrence effect on higher educated employees. This result suggests that clearly articulating what is and is not acceptable is very important for "uneducated" employees but doesn't make much difference to college graduates. If the latter are going to be trust violators, the presence of a formal code of ethics simply won't stop them. In fact, they believe that breaking the code is less serious than the fraud itself. Once they decide to be dishonest, it appears that nothing short of a lack of opportunity will stand in their way.

Table 26

Significance of Education Level and Company Factors

Factor	P-Value
Competent Personnel	.007*
Unrealistic Productivity Expectations	.022*
Conflict-of-Interest Statement Not Required	.035*
Department Operated on "Crisis-Management" Basis	.063
Adequate Documents and Records	.090
Independent Checks on Performance	.097
Disclosure of Personal Investments	.111
Department Not Frequently Reviewed	.125
Excessive Trust in Key Employee	.251
Failure to Discipline Policy Violators	.266
Inadequate Background Check Before Employment	.294
Pay Not Commensurate with Responsibility	.323
Budget Review Lacking	.371
Records of Discipline	.464
Attention to Detail	.495
Not Informed of Company Policy	.632
Separation of Custody from Accounting	.665
Clear Lines of Authority	.727
Department Lacked Budgeted Operation	.746
Separation of Accounting Function Duties	.747
Proper Procedures for Authorization	.791
Separation of Authorization and Recording of Transactions	.852
Department Inadequately Staffed	.907
Clearly Defined Personnel Policies	.919
Inadequate Physical Security	.945

* = Significant at .05 level.

Salary vs. Perpetrator Factors

The fourth set of cross-correlations involved those where salary level was examined to see what impact it had on other factors. In order to compute significance levels, perpetrators were classified into four salary groups: less than $10,000 per year, $10,000 - $20,000, $20,000 - $40,000, and more than $40,000. Table 27 shows there are ten perpetrator factors where salary level appears to make a significant difference.

Of these ten factors, five are such that a higher salary is more

Table 27
Significance of Salary and Perpetrator Factors

Factor	P-Value
Close Association With Suppliers	.000*
Supported Extramarital Relationships	.001*
A Wheeler Dealer	.001*
A Criminal Record	.007*
Expensive Automobiles	.007*
Extensive Involvement in Speculative Investments	.007*
Poor Credit Rating	.012*
New/Remodeled Home	.015*
Recreation Property	.039*
Drug Problems	.042*
Living Beyond Means	.075
Overwhelming Desire for Personal Gain	.093
Lacked Personal Stability	.132
Extravagant Wardrobe	.140
High Personal Debt	.165
Challenged to Beat System	.172
Close Association with Customers	.201
Undue Family/Peer Pressure	.210
Extravagant Vacations	.263
Feeling of Job Dissatisfaction	.274
Excessive Gambling Habits	.280
No Time off Longer Than 2-3 Days	.366
Continually Threatening to Quit	.384
Alcohol Problems	.450
Lack Recognition of Job Performance	.452
Felt Pay Not Commensurate With Responsibility	.589
Believed Job in Jeopardy	.603
Rationalized Poor Performance	.744
A Civil-Suit Defendant	.800
Provided Unreliable Communications	.922
Severe Personal Financial Loss	.957

* = Significant at .05 level.

likely associated with fraud than a lower salary. They are:
1. Close association with suppliers.
2. Having extramarital relationships.
3. Being a wheeler dealer.
4. Having extensive speculative investments.
5. Purchasing recreation property.

The first, "close association with suppliers," suggests that lower-paid employees don't deal much with suppliers; thus, the kind of fraud that such relationships allow is usually unavailable to them. The other three, dealing with extramarital relationships, speculative investments, and recreation property, appear to be amenities enjoyed by only the high-salaried employees. Each can be prohibitively expensive, so it is not unusual to learn that even someone with high salary can get into financial troubles. Because a need for money to support these habits cannot be made public, some employees will resort to fraudulent activities to secure needed money.

Four of the remaining significant factors have inverse relationship with salary level. Specifically, having a criminal record, drug problems, poor credit rating, and buying expensive automobiles are usually associated with lower-salaried employees who commit fraud. These results are often attributed to the fact that higher-salaried employees don't have these specific problems or that having these problems isn't enough to motivate them to commit fraud. Our findings also show that high-salaried employees are more enamoured with extramarital relationships, speculative investments, and recreation property.

The final significant perpetrator factor, "purchasing a new home or remodeling an existing home," is a motivating factor for those employees earning between $10,000 and $20,000. Perhaps those persons making less money don't worry about housing, and those earning more can afford to legitimately increase their standard of living by remodeling or moving.

Salary vs. Company Factors

Table 28 shows there are six company or environmental factors where salary appears to make a difference. They include "failure to discipline perpetrators," "operating on a crisis basis," "failure to maintain records of discipline," "being in a department that is not frequently reviewed," "lack of budgets," and "not reviewing existing budgets." Each appears to be correlated more with higher-salaried employees and are of the type which en-

52

hances fraud opportunities by creating an opportunity or a feeling that, even if caught, the consequences are not serious. Reason dictates that higher-paid employees have the most to lose if caught in fraudulent activities. With this in mind, we may speculate that they generally will perpetrate fraud only if they believe that they can do so without being caught or without adverse consequences. Thus, in order to ultimately stop the large frauds which are perpetrated by the highest paid and most educated employees, all opportunities must be squelched and those caught must be severely punished.

Company Type vs. Perpetrator Factors

The final set of cross-correlations involves those where various types of companies were analyzed to see if fraud factors are more important in some business settings than in others. To

Table 28
Significance of Salary and Company Factors

Factor	P-Value
Failure to Discipline Policy Violators	.001[*]
Department Operated on "Crisis-Management" Basis	.005[*]
Records of Discipline	.017[*]
Department Not Frequently Reviewed	.030[*]
Department Lacked Budgeted Operations	.043[*]
Budget Review Lacking	.043[*]
Excessive Trust in Key Employee	.060
Conflict-of-Interest Statement Not Required	.063
Unrealistic Productivity Expectations	.083
Adequate Documents and Records	.098
Clearly Defined Personnel Policies	.112
Separation of Custody from Accounting	.118
Pay Not Commensurate with Responsibility	.155
Competent Personnel	.159
Separation of Authorization and Recording of Transactions	.183
Department Inadequately Staffed	.315
Proper Procedures for Authorization	.364
Independent Checks on Performance	.507
Disclosure of Personal Investments	.520
Clear Lines of Authority	.542
Separation of Accounting Function Duties	.713
Inadequate Physical Security	.795
Not Informed of Company Policy	.802
Inadequate Background Check Before Employment	.823
Attention to Detail	.892

[*] = Significant at .05 level.

make these calculations, responding companies were divided into seven industry classifications: educational institutions; financial companies; insurance companies; manufacturing companies; utility companies; retail firms; and others.

Table 29 shows there are five perpetrator factors where company type appears to make a significant difference. The first, "overwhelming desire for personal gain," was most significant in educational institutions. While this was a factor in nearly 86 per-

Table 29
Significance of the Type of Company and Perpetrator Factors

Factor	P-Value
Overwhelming Desire for Personal Gain	.008*
Extravagant Vacations	.009*
Supported Extramarital Relationships	.026*
Drug Problems	.039*
Lacked Personal Stability	.044*
Feeling of Job Dissatisfaction	.097
Recreation Property	.117
Provided Unreliable Communications	.179
Challenged to Beat System	.180
New/Remodeled Home	.184
Undue Family/Peer Pressure	.280
Lack of Recognition of Job Performance	.291
A Wheeler Dealer	.298
Alcohol Problems	.317
Excessive Gambling Habits	.443
Poor Credit Rating	.480
Extensive Involvement in Speculative Investments	.490
Close Association with Customers	.505
Close Association with Suppliers	.536
Expensive Automobiles	.579
A Civil-Suit Defendant	.598
Felt Pay Not Commensurate with Responsibility	.605
A Criminal Record	.610
Continually Threatening to Quit	.675
Extravagant Wardrobe	.676
Rationalized Poor Performance	.730
No Time off Longer Than 2-3 Days	.735
Severe Personal Financial Loss	.773
Living Beyond Means	.798
High Personal Debt	.829
Believed Job in Jeopardy	.958

* = Significant at .05 level.

cent of educational institution frauds, it was a consideration in only 28 percent of the cases in other industries.

"Taking extravagant vacations" was a motivating factor more in manufacturing and other firms but not in education, insurance, financial, utility, or retail companies. Likewise, "supporting extramarital relations" was more commonly listed in educational and manufacturing company frauds. "Drug problems" and "lack of personal stability" earned votes more in financial companies than in others.

Company Type vs. Company Factors

There are 11 company or environmental factors where type of company makes a difference.

Table 30
Significance of the Type of Company
and Company Factors

Factor	P-Value
Inadequate Physical Security	.000*
Department Not Frequently Reviewed	.000*
Attention to Detail	.010*
Separation of Custody from Accounting	.001*
Separation of Authorization and Recording of Transactions	.001*
Conflict-of-Interest Statement Not Required	.001*
Excessive Trust in Key Employee	.007*
Competent Personnel	.013*
Clear Lines of Authority	.037*
Separation of Accounting Function Duties	.039*
Independent Checks on Performance	.043*
Clearly Defined Personnel Policies	.089
Failure to Discipline Policy Violators	.101
Pay Not Commensurate with Responsibility	.151
Records of Discipline	.233
Proper Procedures for Authorization	.240
Inadequate Background Check Before Employment	.276
Department Lacked Budgeted Operation	.297
Adequate Documents and Records	.547
Disclosure of Personal Investments	.565
Unrealistic Productivity Expectations	.572
Department Operated on "Crisis-Management" Basis	.070
Department Inadequately Staffed	.883
Budget Review Lacking	.954
Not Informed of Company Policy	.958

* = Significant at .05 level.

The insurance companies questioned felt strongly that they were lacking in the area of physical security systems and indicated that this contributed to frauds in their industry. The other industries, however, did not perceive this to be a problem.

The second factor, "not frequently reviewed by internal auditors," was listed by about half of the firms – 67 percent from the educational, manufacturing, utility, retail, and others; but only 29 percent of those from the financial and insurance industries agreed. This suggests that internal auditors in financial and insurance firms review more frequently than do their counterparts in the other industries. Almost all respondents felt that more frequent and extensive reviews would be a strong fraud deterrent.

"Not paying adequate attention to detail" was acknowledged as a contributing factor by all responsents, although not as heavily by those in the financial and insurance industries, thus emphasizing the significance of the chi-square statistic.

With the exception of those representing the financial companies, everyone felt that failure to enforce a separation of custody of assets from those accounting for those assets contributed to fraud. This might not be a problem in financial companies because they deal heavily in cash and have probably placed emphasis on controls which call for a separation of duties. Only respondents from the utility companies did not believe that a failure to enforce a separation of authorization of transactions from the custody of related assets contributed to their frauds.

The response to one factor was almost split down the middle. Respondents in the education, utility, retail, and other firms felt strongly that requiring employees to complete conflict-of-interest questionnaires would have deterred their frauds, while participants from financial, insurance, and manufacturing firms did not. We believe this controversy can be attributed directly to the differences in industries – in some, such questionnaires are common, while in others, they are not. For example, a recent survey indicated that almost all financial companies require their employees to complete conflict-of-interest statements on an annual basis.

As was the case with paying inadequate attention to details, 100 percent of the respondents felt that placing too much trust in key individuals contributed to their frauds. The chi-square statistic comes into play because those in the financial and utility companies only "agreed," while all others "strongly" agreed.

Retail and other (mainly service) firms believed that hiring incompetent personnel was a factor in their frauds. This result may be quite logical since these two industries often hire low-paid, inexperienced employees to serve as clerks in their stores and subsequently witness higher turnover. However, most of their reported frauds are small, unsophisticated, and lack any intelligent concealment effort.

Everyone, except those respondents from the insurance industry, felt that failure to enforce clear lines of authority led to fraudulent activities. While we cannot explain this result, we suspect that the insurance industry has a simpler hierarchical structure than do the others; therefore, there may be less overlap of duties and confusion about work responsibilities.

Conclusions

Without question, employee fraud has had a tremendous impact on today's business. A large amount of our economy's resources is committed to the detection and investigation of fraud. The FBI has labeled this white-collar offense "the crime of the '80s." More alarming than recent increases in the number of frauds is the dollar size of frauds. Past research, although helpful in the development of a fraud framework, has done little in the way of providing validated factors which can assist auditors in the deterrence and/or the detection of fraud.

The objective of this study was to validate or dismiss factors from a list of 82 red flags. These warning signals flashed insights into perpetrator situational pressures and opportunities to commit fraud as established by the perpetrator or company. Data was obtained on 212 frauds, and the following presents some of the significant findings of our analysis.

Case Demographics

Fraud Size:

Fifty-seven percent of the cases were less than $40,000.

Twenty-two percent were greater than $100,000.

Collusion

Twenty-nine percent of the cases involved collusion.

Manufacturing, insurance, and retailing company cases involved more collusion.

Only 11 percent of the financial institution cases involved collusion.

Fraud Cause and Detection

The major cause of fraud was a failure to enforce established controls.

A lack of internal control also was a significant cause.

Overriding established controls was not a significant cause.

Eighteen percent of the frauds were detected by internal

audit departments.

Thirty-three percent of the frauds were discovered through anonymous tips, etc.

Eighteen percent were detected by normal operating checks/procedures.

Fraud Amount and Industry Type Correlation

Financial Institutions –

Seventy-two percent of frauds were less than $40,000.

Twenty-three percent of frauds were greater than $100,000.

Insurance –

Forty-six percent of frauds were less than $20,000.

Historical data were gathered on the perpetrator including personal demographic and personality factors. The following charts summarize our study's significant perpetrator results.

Perpetrator's Age and Length of Employment

Seventy-four percent of the perpetrators were between 26-45 years of age.

Only two percent of the perpetrators were older than 55.

Forty-one percent of the perpetrators were employed less than five years.

Seventy-two percent of the perpetrators were employed less than ten years.

"Age of the perpetrator" and "amount of the fraud" showed a statistically significant correlation. In general, the older the perpetrator, the greater the amount of fraud.

Age and Amount

Seventy-six percent of the $100,000 and greater were frauds by perpetrators between the ages of 36-45 years.

Of those perpetrators less than 25 years, 82 percent committed frauds of less than $20,000.

Perpetrators' age was also significantly correlated with the type of industry. Insurance and financial institution perpetrators were younger than those in the other industry categories.

Supervisory positions were held by 59 percent of the perpetrators, while 41 percent were clerical workers. In addition, a significant correlation existed between the type of industry and employment position. The perpetrators in the insurance companies – 67 percent – were clerical. The perpetrator with more education tended to defraud in larger amounts than the less educated perpetrator.

The correlations between perpetrators' sex and other variables were statistically significant. Many of these interesting correlations are summarized below:

Perpetrators' Sex

Forty-one percent of all perpetrators were females.

Male perpetrators made a significantly higher salary; no female perpetrator made over $40,000.

Female fraud amounts were less.

Few females colluded in their frauds.

More males overrode controls than females. More women were prosecuted.

Females were given suspended sentences or probation. A higher percentage of men were incarcerated than women.

When incarcerated, men and women served the same time periods.

Female perpetrators were usually employed for shorter periods of time.

Shown below are ten personality factors in "fact-order" ranking (see Table 14). Note that only the top seven have mean scores above 3.50 (the agree range). The perception score for all the factors was higher than the fact score. This leads us to conclude that few of the personality factors were pervasive across the fraud cases. The audit directors judged information on most of these factors as being available yet most would not gather the information because they felt it was of no value or too costly to obtain on key employees. We must question the perceived lack of value of these factors given the pervasive correlation between the presence of these factors and our sample of 212 frauds.

Perpetrator Characteristics: Ranking by Fact Mean

Perpetrator Characteristics	Fact Mean	Fact Rank	Perception Rank
Living Beyond Means	4.397	1	2
Overwhelming Desire for Personal Gain	4.051	2	14
High Personal Debt	3.938	3	4
Close Association with Customers	3.821	4	15
Believed Pay Not Commensurate	3.811	5	16
Wheeler Dealer	3.791	6	11
Challenge to Beat the System	3.489	7	5
Excessive Gambling Habits	3.312	8	1
Undue Family/Peer Pressure	3.214	9	24

Audit directors listed personal debt, greed, living beyond means, and great temptations as the primary reasons why perpetrators defrauded. The data gathered indicated that most perpetrators spent fraud monies on expensive automobiles, homes, extramarital relationships, vacations, and wardrobes in approximately equal percentages of the time.

Shown below are the 12 company factors in "fact order"

which had a mean score in the agree range (above 3.5). The audit directors perceived that all factors but "requiring investment disclosure" were important (see Table 19).

Organizational Environment: Fact Ranking

Organizational Environment Characteristics	Fact Mean	Fact Rank	Perception Rank
Too Much Trust in Key Employees	4.677	1	9
Lack Proper Procedures for Authorizations	4.480	2	1
Lack Personal Investment Income Disclosure	4.478	3	25
No Separation of Transaction Authorization from Custody	4.299	4	3
No Independent Checks on Performance	4.292	5	7
Lack Adequate Attention to Detail	4.221	6	10
No Separation of Asset Custody from Accounting	4.111	7	2
No Separation of Accounting Duties	3.982	8	4
Lack of Clear Lines of Authority	3.933	9	6
Department Not Frequently Reviewed	3.645	10	14
No Conflict-of-Interest Statement	3.590	11	23
Inadequate Documents and Records	3.565	12	5

The results of the analysis of actions taken against the perpetrator are interesting.

Actions Taken

Only 51 percent were prosecuted.

Ninety-eight percent of those prosecuted were found guilty.

Thirty-one percent were incarcerated.

Fifty-two percent of the incarcerations were for less than two years.

The combined probability of a perpetrator's being prosecuted and serving more than two years in jail was 7.7 percent.

Seventy-two percent of those incarcerated made less than $20,000 – only 12 percent made more than $40,000.

With respect to the cross-correlations, there are a significant number of the perpetrator and company factors where size of fraud, sex, educational level, salary, and type of industry made a difference. The purpose of the cross-correlations was to isolate these effects in an effort to make the results more meaningful. The chart below separates the perpetrator and company factors into those that appear to be correlated with "large" and "small" frauds:

Correlated with Large Frauds

Perpetrator Factors

Using proceeds to purchase a new home or remodel existing home.

Using proceeds to take extravagant vacations.

Using proceeds to purchase expensive automobiles.
Using proceeds to purchase expensive wardrobes.
Using proceeds to purchase recreation property.
Using proceeds to support extramarital relationships.
Intellectually challenged to beat the system.
Extensive involvement in speculative investments.

Company Factors

Lack of separation of custody of assets from the accounting for those assets.
Lack of separation of duties within the accounting function.
Lack of separating authorization of transactions from recording those transactions.
Lack of competent personnel.
Imposing unrealistic productivity expectations.
Operated on a crisis basis.
Placing excessive trust in key employees.

Correlated with Small Frauds

Perpetrator Factors

Feeling that pay is not commensurate with responsibility.

While there were many factors where size of fraud appeared to make a difference, there were very few where perpetrators' sex was a distinguishing characteristic. The following list contains those factors deemed significant.

Correlated with Male Perpetrators

Perpetrator Factors

Wheeler-dealer attitude.
Close association with suppliers.
Feeling of job dissatisfaction.

Company Factors

Operating on a crisis basis.

Correlated with Female Perpetrators

Perpetrator Factors

Lack of personal stability.

The implications from these results are that the fraud detection and the deterrence efforts should be the same for both men and women.

There were seven perpetrator and three company factors where education level of the perpetrator appeared to make a difference. These are summarized as follows:

Higher Education Correlated with Fraud

Perpetrator Factors

Wheeler-dealer attitude.

Close association with suppliers.

Overwhelming desire for personal gain.

Company Factors

Hiring incompetent personnel.

Imposing unrealistic productivity measurements.

Started but Did Not Finish College Correlated with Fraud

Perpetrator Factors

Using proceeds to take extravagant vacations.

Using proceeds to purchase recreation property.

Using proceeds to support extramarital relationships.

Using proceeds to purchase expensive automobiles.

Lesser Education Correlated with Fraud

Company Factors

Not requiring a conflict-of-interest statement.

As indicated in the demographics section, there appears to be a high correlation between education level and salary. Therefore, we would expect a similarity in the results between these two variables. The following chart confirms these similarities, although salary appears to make a difference in more cases than does education level.

High Salary Correlated with Fraud

Perpetrator Factors

Close association with suppliers.

Having extramarital relationships.

Wheeler-dealer attitude.

Having extensive speculative investments.

Purchasing recreation property.

Company Factors

Failure to discipline perpetrators.

Operating on a crisis basis.

Failure to maintain records of discipline.

Not being frequently reviewed.

Lack of budgets.

No review of existing budgets.

Low Salary Correlated with Fraud

Perpetrator Factors

Having a criminal record.

Having drug problems.

Having a poor credit rating.

Buying expensive automobiles.

Company Factors

Not requiring a conflict-of-interest statement.

Living beyond means.

Perpetrator Factors

Purchasing a new or remodeling an existing home.

The final set of cross-correlations involved examining the various industry groups to see if type of company made a significant difference. There were several cases where both perpetrator and company factors were influenced by the type of company. However, because there were seven industry groups and the results varied significantly among the factors, it is difficult to summarize them in chart form as was possible with the other cross-correlations.

PART
2

Case Studies by Industry

The following case studies provide ample insight into the reality of white-collar crime. No industry is left untouched by this rather frightening and fast-growing phenomenon, ranging from the financial institutions to the grand halls of government.

A sampling of case studies was selected from the 212 reports gathered and represents the entire gamut of scams, both sophisticated and simple, involving hundreds of thousands of dollars. Techniques and motivations vary, as do employee-job descriptions, titles, and gender. Each case, however, serves a vital purpose in the context of this presentation: to introduce specific symptoms and systems that should assist internal auditors in detecting and deterring fraud.

It should be noted that these case studies were provided and written by internal auditors who had investigated the frauds and were familiar with them. In order to preserve originality and intent of the case writers, we have printed them as submitted except for minor grammatical corrections.

          Industry: Construction
              Type: Submission of fraudulent invoices for payment
            Amount: $560,000
      Legal Action: Terminated, prosecuted, placed on probation
  Perpetrator's Age: 35
            Gender: Male
Length of Employment: 9 years

The perpetrator was a shipping clerk responsible for sending requested materials to overseas subsidiaries. He also was responsible for approving freight invoices and purchasing minor items for the company warehouse. The employee charged costs to a clearing account and then reconciled it and invoiced the subsidiaries for shipments made.

The employee committed the fraud by submitting false invoices and approving them for payment through the company's centralized accounts payable system. Checks were sent to a private post-office box where they were picked up by an accomplice who converted the checks to cash at a local branch of a bank. The accomplice may possibly have had a bank connection because he did not have an account but was able to cash several checks in excess of $25,000.

The employee covered up the charges by spreading them among various subsidiary shipments and by controlling data requests on clearing account and reconciliation information. Management performed only a perfunctory review of reconciliation. Invoices submitted to accounts payable were all photocopies of supposed "originals." Some invoices were located for transactions showing the actual merchandise purchased but were then modified on the photocopies to appear as items required by the companies. Purchase order copies and receiving documents were maintained in outlying locations and were not sent to central accounts payable; thus, control was unavailable.

No in-house accomplice was discovered. The employee was very creative and tested the system with small purchases before moving on to significant sums.

Industry:	Construction
Type:	Theft of inventory and materials from construction site
Amount:	$5,000
Legal Action:	None; disciplined
Perpetrator's Age:	45
Gender:	Male
Length of Employment:	15 years

A large international construction company had a remote project in the Southwest. The project was understaffed with respect to supervisory personnel; and as a result, one individual ordered, received, and supervised the warehousing of a variety of materials. This long-time employee misappropriated building materials, auto parts, and other goods over a period of about six months. He ordered excess material which he received and removed from the site. The project staff were all long-time employees but apparently did not question the discrepancies. During a regular audit, a relatively new employee brought the problem to the attention of the audit department.

Industry: Education
Type: Bid-rigging and overstatement of payroll hours
Amount: Unknown
Legal Action: Unknown
Perpetrator's Age: Unknown
Gender: Male
Length of Employment: Unknown

The payroll fraud was perpetrated by a supervisor and involved the collusion of part-time subordinates who feared for their jobs if they did not participate in the fraud. The supervisor had subordinates sign time cards and turn them over to him. He then filled in the hours and added extra hours above those actually worked. The supervisor then approved them and sent them to the business office for processing. He picked up the checks, wrote on the stub the value of the extra hours, and then distributed them to his workers. They were instructed to return cash to him for the amount of the extra hours.

The supervisor was also involved in a bid-rigging situation which allowed him to receive kickbacks for equipment ordered for his department. Because of poor communications between all the associated departments and the supervisor, no legal action was taken. This fraud was perpetrated because of misinterpretation of the conflict-of-interest statutes by a responsible individual, poor communication between departments, and the considerable influence exerted over the items purchased by the supervisor because of his expertise.

Industry: Education
Type: Cashing paychecks not picked up by employees
Amount: $1,200
Legal Action: Terminated, decision on prosecution pending
Perpetrator's Age: 43
Gender: Female
Length of Employment: 7 years

Approximately one month after the payroll check date, Mr. Smith attempted to pick up his check from Ms. Doe, who was responsible for all departmental check distributions. Ms. Doe stated that the check was lost and that she would process the necessary data to obtain a new check. She then entered false payroll data in order to generate the check. Within a few weeks, a new check was received by Mr. Smith. However, upon checking his year-to-date earnings, he discovered that the "lost" check amount was included as earned income. When confronted with the situation, Ms. Doe admitted to her supervisor that she had forged Mr. Smith's name and cashed the check for personal reasons.

An audit of departmental business activities produced three additional fraud cases. Lack of separation of duties was the primary cause; Ms. Doe exercised complete control over departmental business activities, and all cases involved payroll checks that were not promptly picked up by employees. Ms. Doe kept the checks on file; and when it appeared the employees had forgotten about their earnings, she cashed the checks. If at a later date employees requested payment, she processed false data to generate payments in the appropriate amounts. Other business activities under her control were audited; but due to inadequate record keeping, fraudulent activities could not be verified.

Industry:	Education
Type:	Creation of fictitious employees, submission of fictitious billings
Amount:	$14,699
Legal Action:	Terminated, prosecuted, placed on probation
Perpetrator's Age:	41
Gender:	Female
Length of Employment:	15 years

Sue Ellen was a department head with supervising responsibilities for budget, purchasing, payroll, revenue depositing, etc. She gradually altered procedures, eliminating separation of duties until she had full control of all office activities. For example, she initiated hiring documents, verified and approved hourly wages and amounts of wages, and attested to the payroll accuracy of time-slip employees. She signed all purchasing documents and instructed mail clerks to route all business office mail to her unopened.

Once she had assumed full responsibility, she "hired" fictitious personnel. She opened an "unofficial" bank account and deposited payroll checks accordingly. The account was opened in the same bank that had the agency's official account and was given a similar title. Sue Ellen was the sole authorized signatory.

She authorized and initiated payment from agency funds for purchases made by an affiliated organization which had also made payments on the same purchases. When vendor refunds were received, she deposited the checks to the unofficial bank account. She assumed full responsibility for depositing revenue received throughout the agency; a portion of the revenue was diverted to the unofficial account.

The fraud was revealed when the perpetrator was ill and when the replacement verifying the time-slip payroll did not recognize the names of the employees.

Industry: Education
Type: Misappropriation of tuition payments using a lapping scheme and double entries to records
Amount: $66,000
Legal Action: Terminated, pursued prosecution, but grand jury did not indict
Perpetrator's Age: 29
Gender: Female
Length of Employment: 6.5 years

This fraud occurred at one of several campus cashier's offices maintained by the university for the collection and processing of student tuition bills and other related charges. The office also receives funds from other university departments which it processes and deposits to its local bank account.

The office was staffed by a teller, a head cashier, and some part-time clerical help. The head cashier was responsible for supervising the entire cashiering operation in addition to functioning as a teller when needed. The cashier's office and adjacent (student) accounts receivable office were the responsibility of one manager. Although the two offices perform separate functions, a great amount of cross-referencing is involved with a common need for the same information. The coordination of functions was the manager's responsibility; an ideal internal control situation would have restricted access to both offices to only the manager. However, the head cashier had access to the accounts receivable records.

The perpetrator was employed as a teller for approximately five years before being promoted to head cashier. This position called for the reconciliation of the daily cash register receipts to the cash transmittals and bank deposits plus the preparation of deposits for funds received from outside departments such as the bookstore or dining service operations. These deposits involved substantial amounts of cash. As head cashier, she also prepared the initial accounting documents that serve as the input to the various general ledger accounts.

The perpetrator's extensive knowledge and experience, coupled with the trust placed in her by the manager, resulted in a diminishing review of her work, particularly the cash register reconciliations. She soon was able to manipulate the documentation and the control procedures necessary to conceal the continued embezzlement of funds. She was also able to anticipate the demands of the other areas of the office and could satisfy their needs without significant shortages becoming readily apparent.

Each transaction for a student payment involves the receipt of cash or check and a credit to the individual's receivable account on a subsidiary ledger. Each aspect of the transaction has its own internal control check. The cash receipts must match the cash register control totals, and the A/R credits should equal the bank deposits; ideally, they can be reconciled back to the total cash receipts.

The majority of the losses were the result of tuition payments being misappropriated, although some cash payments were taken outright. Checks were converted to cash by substituting them for cash, usually in one of the outside deposits. In many instances, checks were substituted for more recent checks several times before the opportunity arose for her to remove cash.

The perpetrator attempted to credit the receivable accounts of the individual students whose payments she had misappropriated in two different ways. The initial method was used during the period when the office was processing payment cards through a batch process. She submitted two different batches of bills – one bogus and one legitimate – but made only one bank deposit. This was done twice during the embezzlement, each time as the batch processing period was ending.

The other method of crediting the receivable accounts resembled a lapping operation. The perpetrator credited an individual's receivable account only when it was about to become delinquent. She would use whatever funds she collected on that day to support the delayed credits. She would also use money collected from any miscellaneous charges or accounts already past due to cover the previously misappropriated funds.

It was not known how she expected to hide these shortages at year-end when a comprehensive reconciliation would be performed by someone outside her department, for it was shortly before this time when the fraud was discovered.

Industry: Education
Type: Obtained unauthorized airline tickets by colluding with travel agency
Amount: $2,500
Legal Action: Terminated, prosecuted, placed on probation
Perpetrator's Age: 40
Gender: Male
Length of Employment: 4 years

A professor doing research on worldwide earthquake predictions was having an extramarital relationship with his secretary. Through collusion with a travel agent, he obtained an airline ticket for his secretary for a foreign trip; her ticket was not authorized by the federal grant, so he billed the trip as domestic travel. The travel agency paid from the invoice and the university made no cross check between tickets and the invoice. However, the agency later questioned it and brought it to the attention of university officials. Once the university obtained a guilty confession from the professor, restitution was made. But he was placed on probation and was terminated by the university.

Industry: Education
Type: Theft of cash
Amount: $17,500
Legal Action: Terminated, prosecution initiated, but dropped
Perpetrator's Age: 23
Gender: Female
Length of Employment: 2.5 years

An employee in food services received daily receipts from sales along with the cash-register tapes from two-three cashiers. The employee ensured that the tapes were mutilated and could not be read. She prepared the transmittal of funds to the comptroller but kept the difference between the amount transmitted and submitted to her by the cashiers. She sent the mutilated tapes to the comptroller with the deposit. The comptroller's office did not compare the deposit with the cash-register tapes.

The fraud was detected when one of the cashiers noted the transmittal to the comptroller was small for a comparatively busy day. When questioned about tracing the transmittal amount to the cash register tapes, the perpetrator could not show completed tapes.

An audit examination covering approximately one to one-and-a-half years prior to the discovery date was considered. The estimated loss set at $17,500 was determined by analyzing the deposits and available cash-register tapes.

Industry: Education
Type: Use of blanket purchase order for personal item
Amount: $988
Legal Action: Terminated, prosecuted, placed on probation
Perpetrator's Age: 31
Gender: Female
Length of Employment: 1 year

Betty was a clerk who observed that department personnel occasionally used blanket-purchase orders to buy miscellaneous items at local stores. In violation of approved policy, blanket orders were presigned by the authorizing party (several at a time) and were kept in an unlocked file cabinet. Betty saw the opportunity to use the blanket orders for personal use and proceeded to purchase food items, cat food, etc.

Prior to the discovery, Betty moved to a different department. However, her former department uncovered the loss when expenditure documents were being reviewed. Betty was confronted and made restitution through her lawyer. When Betty's new supervisor learned of her past history, he wanted to fire her because her position gave her signature authority on blanket-purchase orders. When he discussed the situation with the personnel department, the supervisor was erroneously told that he had no choice but to keep her in this position.

Shortly after she was hired, Betty signed blanket-purchase orders and once again made purchases from local stores for personal use. The fraud was discovered when Betty was seen making purchases with a blanket-purchase order by a member of the internal audit staff.

Industry: Education
Type: Using company personnel to do perpetrator's consulting
Amount: $30,000
Legal Action: Terminated, prosecuted, trial pending
Perpetrator's Age: 40
Gender: Male
Length of Employment: 10 years

An employee used university resources for personal gain. He had worked in another campus department, and it was assumed he knew the rules. The employee had experienced similar problems in a previous department, but no disciplinary action was taken. It had been handled "informally," and no adverse personnel action was recorded. As a faculty member, he had a great deal of management responsibility. The employee had research staff under his direction working on his private consulting and had led them to believe it was an approved project. He got into trouble when his funded research ran out of money long before completion.

The employees performing the unauthorized work did not complain for fear of losing their jobs. The unique nature of his work, the lack of closer progress monitoring by his peers, and his ability to "talk a good line" prevented earlier disclosure. The employee was charged in court with theft of services and is awaiting trial.

The formal investigation which led to court action was initiated after the university learned in the newspaper of his consulting service and started asking questions. While this occurred at a university, any research facility that does not closely monitor projects could potentially become victim of such an activity.

Industry: Education
Type: Voiding cash register receipt entries, pocketing cash
Amount: $7,500
Legal Action: Terminated, not prosecuted
Perpetrator's Age: 27
Gender: Male
Length of Employment: 4 years

The cashier worked a 4:30-7:30 p.m. shift with few customers. There were three other employees and one manager in the two-story retail business. The cashier was separate from other cashiers at a jewelry and calculator counter. He had his own cash drawer and was responsible for daily balancing.

Periodically, after a customer paid cash for a purchase, he would void the transaction immediately after the customer would leave and later in the shift, as recorded on the cash register, audit tapes. No managerial review of voids was required or made. The accountant who was aware of the excessive quantity of voids just assumed the perpetrator was a poor cash-register operator.

Industry: Financial
Type: Account names, numbers and signature cards given to outsiders
Amount: $3,500
Legal Action: Terminated, prosecution desired but refused by U.S. Attorney
Perpetrator's Age: 20
Gender: Female
Length of Employment: 8 months

A check file clerk in account records was providing the account number, names, and signatures on card copy for accounts with balances in excess of $5,000. This information was passed along to her father who, along with several of his friends, presented split deposit transactions against the accounts provided.

Since the cash back was only 10 percent of the account balance and the signatures appeared authentic, the tellers paid $3,500 in cash on forged items over a three-day period.

The fraud was discovered when the statements were sent to the customers four weeks later. The clerk had selected accounts which would receive statements a month later.

Industry: Financial
Type: Credit card fraud
Amount: $9,413
Legal Action: Terminated, prosecuted, placed on probation
Perpetrator's Age: 20
Gender: Female
Length of Employment: 1 year

The new accounts clerk was given the responsibility of maintaining computer pregenerated credit-card account numbers and generating the input form. Once accounts were activated, she was responsible for reviewing input. With the fictitious cards, she and a friend were able to obtain funds from the ATMs as well as make purchases at area stores.

When the fictitious accounts became delinquent and were researched, it was discovered that there were no signed applications. This led to the subsequent finding of the forgeries. The subject was charged with one count of felony misuse of a credit card, placed in the diversion program, and is now making restitution payments to the courts.

In retrospect, this situation could have been prevented by a separation of duties. If one person is responsible for generating input to a system, someone else should be responsible for reviewing the work generated by the system.

Industry:	Financial
Type:	Directing funds in large, seldom used accounts to perpetrator's use
Amount:	$55,000
Legal Action:	Terminated, prosecuted, placed on probation
Perpetrator's Age:	55
Gender:	Female
Length of Employment:	20 years

The teller was a long-time trusted employee and well-known resident who had worked for the bank 20 years. Prior to a merger with another bank, she had been the "savings teller" and had good relationships with many customers. She and her husband had a son who had been giving them much difficulty. When the fraud occurred, it was learned that the son – who was known by local law-enforcement officers – was a practicing homosexual with a severe drug problem.

The teller selected about 20 elderly customers, all of whom had passbook savings accounts with large balances. It was later revealed that the teller would stop by the customers' homes to pick up and deliver passbooks, making transactions as requested, but withdrawing monies over a two-year period. She made false transactions and altered others.

The fraud was accidentally detected when the teller inadvertently used the wrong account number on a deposit ticket. When the customer informed the branch manager, the latter recognized the teller's writing and grew suspicious because teller preparation of customer deposit tickets is prohibited. Subsequently, an internal audit was called to investigate the situation, which uncovered a series of unauthorized entries, etc.

Industry: Financial
Type: Diversion of cash and customer funds
Amount: $2,915.61
Legal Action: Case remanded to FBI
Perpetrator's Age: Unknown
Gender: Unknown
Length of Employment: Unknown

The subject took money from the teller fund for which he was responsible. To conceal the resulting shortage, he falsified cash reports, processed fabricated cash-outs, or intercepted checks. His activities were discovered when a customer who deposited a check complained about not having been credited.

The case was remanded to the FBI and full restitution was made.

Industry: Financial
Type: Diversion of teller-cage funds; stealing from other employees; forgery
Amount: $5,000
Legal Action: Charged with one count of felonious forgery; placed in diversion program
Perpetrator's Age: Unknown
Gender: Unknown
Length of Employment: 11 months

The subject observed other tellers opening their teller cash vaults and memorized the combinations. Later, when it was convenient, he opened the other tellers' vaults, removed money, and relocked the safes.

The subject processed customer deposits as usual. However, on some days when he needed money, fraudulent counter checks or savings-withdrawal slips were processed. The subject pocketed the differences which caused an overage of the teller's cage. Also, the subject removed bills from "strapped money."

When customers realized that additional, unauthorized transactions were made to their accounts, they reported such and filed affidavits. This led to an investigation which indicated the subject's involvement.

When confronted with the evidence, the subject confessed the forgeries; subsequent inquiry resulted in further admissions. The subject was charged with one count of felonious forgery, placed in the diversion program, and had made one payment at the time of this report.

Industry: Financial
Type: Diverting cash from a night deposit
Amount: $1,050
Legal Action: Terminated; charges filed, pending trial
Perpetrator's Age: Unknown
Gender: Unknown
Length of Employment: 13 months

A teller processed a customer's night-deposit bag, issued a receipt and took $1,050 in cash from the deposit. The checks and remaining cash were hidden in the teller's cage.

During an investigation involving a similar disappearance, management searched the teller's cage and discovered the unprocessed deposit which was short cash. A subsequent audit showed that the cage balanced without the deposit, thereby confirming that the deposit was short.

The subject was terminated; charges have been filed.

Industry: Financial
Type: Diverting cash from night-depository bags
Amount: $1,130
Legal Action: Charged with felony; recommended for diversion program
Perpetrator's Age: Unknown
Gender: Unknown
Length of Employment: Unknown

A teller who processed night deposits would often take cash if the customer listed the cash for a lesser amount than was enclosed.

Numerous customer complaints prompted office management to set up a dummy account. When confronted with resulting evidence, the suspect confessed. The subject was charged with a felony, recommended for the diversion program, and is now making restitution payments to the local courts.

Industry: Financial
Type: Embezzlement of bank funds
Amount: $465
Legal Action: Terminated
Perpetrator's Age: 20
Gender: Female
Length of Employment: 2 years

The collections department, in the process of following up on a delinquent mortgage, had a dispute with a customer as to whether a certain payment had been made. The customer held a stamped receipt for payment, but the bank had no correlative record of payment. The customer had gone into a branch, purchased a money order made payable to the bank, and used it to make payment on his mortgage. Since the customer was making a late payment, it could not be processed on-line; so the money order and coupon were forwarded to the loan operations area.

Research into the discrepancy by an employee of the collections department proved that the money order had been deposited into the personal account of a loan-operations clerk. When the person in question was interrogated, she admitted having taken the money order, but said she had paid back the money. That afternoon, she stole a draft from her department, entered the deposit-operations area and made unauthorized use of the terminal to process the loan payment. When the terminal operator did not balance, she was told that the suspect had used the terminal earlier that day. When questioned, the perpetrator said she only used the terminal to make an inquiry on the account. She later brought in a mortgage payment coupon, and the terminal operator balanced.

When the audit department was informed, transactions were investigated regarding her personal accounts. This led to the finding that she had been withdrawing funds on her mother's personal account which she later tried to repay but never did.

She was immediately dismissed from the bank, and arrangements for repayment of the embezzled funds were made through a weekly plan.

Industry: Financial
Type: Embezzlement of cash and securities
Amount: $210,700
Legal Action: Perpetrator resigned before discovery of fraud; prosecuted, sentenced to 30 days and restitution
Perpetrator's Age: 30
Gender: Male
Length of Employment: 5 years

The fraud, perpetrated by a former assistant trust officer at the bank, was multidimensional in nature. The perpetrator utilized existing procedures for his own benefit while defrauding the trust department of $210,700 in securities, chattel, property, income checks, trust-department checks, and tuition reimbursement. This fraud spanned approximately two-and-a-half years. Because of his position as trust officer, he was entrusted with single custody of trust assets on occasion to facilitate the beneficiaries.

On several occasions, the officer requested trust checks be drawn payable to the bank. Utilizing the existing check issuance procedures, these checks were signed by the officer and given to him in direct violation of established procedures. He then utilized these funds to pay personal outstanding debts owed the bank and obtained funds via automatic tellers or by purchasing cashiers checks.

The trust officer utilized the existing securities-distribution system to have securities registered in another bank's name and delivered to him. He subsequently deposited the securities into his own trust account at the bank instead of the distributee account and forged a receipt from the trust officer in charge of the distributee's account.

The trust officer withdrew personal property from the vault for specific accounts and sold it for personal gain. Also, in the distribution of chattel property from an estate, the trust officer was to deliver this property to the beneficiaries under single custody. For property unclaimed, the trust officer sold it for personal gain and fraudulently changed the records to indicate proper disposition.

Due to the nature of the existing bank mail system, mail containing income checks due trust accounts is directly received by trust officers. The perpetrator took checks erroneously made payable to the bank and himself as trustee and utilized them to pay off personal debts held at the bank. Since some of the beneficiaries of these accounts did not receive statements, the fraud went undetected. Also, in some cases the officer utilized a system code which deleted transactions from appearing on the beneficiary statements. His knowledge of the competency of these beneficiaries enabled him to utilize this method of obtaining funds without detection.

The trust officer also submitted copies of altered grade reports in order to receive tuition reimbursement from the bank. He registered for the course, withdrew, and then altered and photocopied grade reports to obtain reimbursement within the established procedures.

Industry:	Financial
Type:	Embezzlement of funds and lapping
Amount:	$10,000
Legal Action:	Terminated, prosecuted, placed on probation
Perpetrator's Age:	50
Gender:	Female
Length of Employment:	26 years

The perpetrator was a receptionist for safe-deposit boxes and a clerk for federal tax deposits. Checks and cards were sent to her, and she prepared the transmittal forms for the IRS and mailed them. Unknown to management, she also accepted Christmas-Club payments from some businessmen who were old friends. They paid in cash, and she held their books. She pocketed the cash and used tax-deposit checks to cover the payments when she received them in even amounts. Her substitute was instructed just to hold the Christmas-Club payments until she returned.

Most tax-deposit checks were covered by lapping. Of those that weren't, she waited until the customer brought in the IRS letter and then typed a fictitious transmittal and sent a copy to IRS, which never challenged them. The fraud was detected when one customer brought the letter and cancelled check to another officer who did his own investigation and discovered it had been applied to Christmas Clubs instead. He informed the internal audit director, who took it from there. The perpetrator refused to cooperate in any way and wouldn't tell bank officials the total amount of the embezzlement.

Industry: Financial
Type: Embezzlement using various holding
accounts
Amount: $194,120
Legal Action: Terminated, prosecuted,
placed on probation
Perpetrator's Age: 32
Gender: Male
Length of Employment: 7 years

A bank branch manager used various holding accounts to conceal a gradually increasing embezzlement totalling $194,120 over a four-year period. Funds were obtained via fraudulent cashier's checks, money orders, and direct deposits to his own accounts. The offsets were charged to a bank-wide interoffice account as loans pending documentation completion.

Periodically, the shortages would be shifted to the branch's cash-items account, but the poorly controlled interoffice account was used most of the time. The method involved clearing the prior entries and offsetting them with new interoffice account entries of differing amounts and descriptions.

The interoffice account was maintained in accounting on a computer system similar to a check reconciling account. Reports indicated how many days items were outstanding. However, bank-wide volume discouraged concentrated follow-up; most often, the issuer was contacted after an excessive period; and his promise to clear the items was all that was necessary. No controls existed to detect situations in which the issuer was also the offsetter. Detection occurred only when repeated delays involving large amounts aroused suspicion.

Industry: Financial
Type: Embezzling portions of death claim
benefits, misstating benefits to
beneficiaries
Amount: $32,300
Legal Action: Terminated, prosecuted, sentenced to
3 years, 3 months of which 3 years
was suspended
Perpetrator's Age: 32
Gender: Female
Length of Employment: 3 years

The employee of a credit union prepared death-claim benefits for deceased members. By use of debit/credit vouchers issued against general ledger accrual accounts, she was appropriating portions of the claims to her own account directly or through her children's and mother's accounts. Death benefits were misstated to the beneficiaries.

Employee used reversing entries to transfer funds from member accounts. Statements for these accounts were intercepted and typed statements substituted. The employee – who was well liked and enjoyed outstanding rapport with members – misappropriated funds from accounts of those 75 years and over who were recently involved in a loss of spouse and were generally unaware of their benefits.

The accounting department prepared gross entries at month-end to balance general ledger accrued term-deposit interest to computer-generated figures with no investigation of amounts involved. Employee transferred small funds from accrued interest to her personal or family's accounts which were lost in the gross month-end adjustments. Approval signatures for the vouchers were obtained from supervisory personnel not directly connected with her work or from direct seniors on busy days when they would initial without investigation.

Activity reports for days she performed illegal transactions were intercepted by her and destroyed. Whenever possible, system entries were entered on a terminal signed on by someone else to reduce the chance of her own account entries being noticed.

Industry:	Financial
Type:	Embezzling tuition refunds
Amount:	$1,800
Legal Action:	Terminated, but not prosecuted
Perpetrator's Age:	38
Gender:	Female
Length of Employment:	20 years

The vice president and personnel officer was responsible for administering the bank's tuition-reimbursement policy. Periodically, department personnel were responsible for ensuring that a grade report was on file for each course an employee had taken. A clerk became suspicious of the vice president when she noticed that no grade reports were filed for courses she had supposedly taken and for which she had been reimbursed. Each time she asked for the grade reports, she was ignored.

The clerical associate reported her suspicion to the internal auditors. They called the college and determined that the officer had indeed signed up for six courses but had dropped them either before or immediately after the first class. She had been reimbursed for all of the courses.

Additional investigation involving the school administrator found that the vice president had dropped the first two courses after one class. The administrator had given the vice president full credit of $300, even though it was against established policy. The perpetrator used the $300 credit to obtain receipts for two more courses the next semester, which were once again dropped with the $300 credit restored. The scenario was repeated one more time.

When confronted with the evidence, the bank officer appeared shocked and refused to confess. She insisted that the money had been returned to the bank. She was terminated, and the $300 credit remains outstanding.

Industry:	Financial
Type:	False entries to bank accounts, fictitious loans, etc.
Amount:	$250,000
Legal Action:	Terminated, prosecuted, sentenced to 5 years
Perpetrator's Age:	40
Gender:	Male
Length of Employment:	15 years

A $250,000 fraud was perpetrated at an autonomous branch bank by one employee. Methods used were false entries to bank accounts, fictitious loans, and fictitious cash items. Fraud was facilitated by an inadequate proof system, ready access to cash, and a lack of segregation of duties. The perpetrator had ready access to cash and loan records and performed daily balancing and accounting functions and reconciled bank accounts. The fraud was discovered during the course of an audit when a reconcilement not received by the auditor on a timely basis raised the suspicion of management.

Industry: Financial
Type: Falsification of bank records
Amount: $30
Legal Action: Unknown.
Perpetrator's Age: Unknown
Gender: Unknown
Length of Employment: Unknown

An account reconciler "purchased" a bank money order made payable to and signed by himself. The "funds" used to purchase the money order were a debit to a cash-item account. The money order was then cashed and deposited into the subject's associate checking account.

The teller who made the transaction reported the irregularity to his supervisor. An investigation ensued, and the subject admitted his guilt and made full restitution.

Industry.: Financial
Type: Falsification of bank records
Amount: $7,909.39
Legal Action: Case remanded to the FBI
Perpetrator's Age: Unknown
Gender: Unknown
Length of Employment: Unknown

The subject received checks returned NSF from foreign correspondent bank-cash letters and resubmitted the checks for payment with the offset being a credit to the subject's demand-deposit account. The subject then generated fictitious general book entries to area banks to cover up the reversals of the original entries.

A review of the due-from-banks account showed that these items were still outstanding after several months. This prompted research led to the investigation and subsequent revelation. The FBI is investigating.

Industry: Financial
Type: Falsifying documents to qualify
marginal real estate buyers
Amount: $0 (to the financial institution)
Legal Action: Terminated, not prosecuted
Perpetrator's Age: 45
Gender: Male
Length of Employment: 10 months

The fraud was perpetrated by a commissioned loan originator for a mortgage-banking company. He worked in a three-person satellite office located about 75 miles from one of the company's branches. All loan processing and reviews were done by satellite personnel, so the branch manager only involved himself to a limited extent.

Both the perpetrator and the local realtors in the area consistently ignored FHA, VA, and HUD regulations requiring employment verifications and deposits of loan applicants. They allowed applicants to hand-carry verifications rather than mail them directly to and from the mortgage company's office.

The loan processor in the satellite office received orders from the perpetrator and allowed him to work on several of his own loan files. This was in direct conflict and violation of company policy.

The fraud consisted of changing information on verifications of employment and deposits of loan applicants. It entailed recopying the information and forging the signature of the person verifying the information. This was usually done where the applicant status was marginal, allowing them to qualify for FHA or VA mortgages.

The forged verifications seemed to fall into four general categories: (1) The applicant's current salary or bonus information was increased to provide sufficient income to qualify for the loan; (2) if the applicant had held several short-term jobs over the previous two years, all but one was discarded and the remaining was changed to make it appear that the applicant was employed by one company for two years in order to establish job stability; (3) account balances were increased to show additional assets; and (4) the account balance and loan balance figures were switched. For example, instead of an actual loan balance of $2,500 and an account balance of $300, the verification would show an account balance of $2,500 and a loan balance of $300.

In the perpetrator's eyes, everyone benefitted from his action. The borrowers qualified for the loan and could buy their house; the realtor made a sale; the mortgage company made a loan; and the perpetrator collected a commission.

The fraud was discovered during a regular internal audit of the branch office. One of the procedures used was to reverify employment samples and deposit verifications by sending a photocopy to the employer or depository. The original sample included three to five loans of each originator. One of the employment verifications from the perpetrator's loans was returned, revealing that the job title, salary, and length of employment were all incorrect and that the person signing the verification did so without authority. The sample was expanded to include ten more loans from each originator. The results showed several exceptions, all from those loans originated by the perpetrator. This called for a full investigation over the nine months the originator had been employed. Approximately one-third of the loans he had granted were done so illegally.

When confronted, the perpetrator flatly denied any knowledge of the fraud and, at various times, accused applicants, realtors, and others of wrongdoing or attributed the evidence to error or coincidence. Loan-processing procedures were followed to the letter in that branch office following this experience.

Industry: Financial
Type: Falsifying invoices and then approving them
Amount: $80,000
Legal Action: Terminated, not prosecuted
Perpetrator's Age: 40
Gender: Male
Length of Employment: 15 years

The perpetrator, a senior officer in the company, falsified and approved invoices, thus causing payments totalling aproximately $80,000 to be paid to fictitious persons. He requested that the checks be returned to him for delivery. He then endorsed the checks as if the fictitious payees had signed and endorsed them to him as a third party. He deposited the checks in his bank account.

To the company's knowledge, no collusion was involved as he was authorized to approve invoices of the type and amounts he falsified. The embezzlement was uncovered when the accounting department was unable to obtain Social Security numbers for the fictitious payees. Accounting personnel reported a lack of cooperation from the perpetrator. Internal audit investigated and uncovered the fraud.

Industry: Financial
Type: Falsifying loan applications
Amount: $7,800
Legal Action: Terminated, prosecution pending
Perpetrator's Age: 35
Gender: Male
Length of Employment: 3 years

A loan officer in a branch bank went on a two-week mandatory vacation. His request to split his vacation was declined by the branch manager. During the second week, a loan trainee noticed that a borrower's delinquency notice had been placed on the officer's desk. The trainee remembered seeing a delinquent notice on the same borrower the previous month. He was unable to locate the borrower's loan file and so advised the branch manager. The file was subsequently located together with others in the absent officer's desk.

The manager was unable to confirm any of the references or credit information in the delinquent loan file, although the officer indicated he had checked the references. Either the references were misplaced or they had been contacted and had no knoeledge of the borrower. The same thing occured with two or three other loan files in the officer's desk, which prompted the manager to contact the auditing division.

A thorough investigation was made of all loans made by the officer. Six fictitious borrowers were found in his loan portfolio with outstanding balances totaling $7,800. The loan officer was interrogated following his vacation and admitted to falsifying the documents.

He had taken the loan proceeds in cash to meet living expenses and to make installment payments on the other loans as they became due. He was immediately terminated, and the fraud was reported to the FBI and the U.S. Attorney for prosecution. The outcome is still pending.

Industry: Financial
Type: Forgery
Amount: $150
Legal Action: Charged with forgery; awaiting trial
Perpetrator's Age: Unknown
Gender: Unknown
Length of Employment: Unknown

The subject waited on a customer and processed a legitimate transaction. Later in the day, he took a savings withdrawal from this customer's account, filled it out for $150, and forged a signature; however, the signature was that of an unauthorized employee.

The customer signed an affidavit charging forgery. This initiated an investigation which indicted the subject as being the instigator. The perpetrator was charged with forgery and is awaiting trial.

Industry: Financial
Type: Forgery
Amount: $7,000
Legal Action: Case remanded to FBI; bound over
to the grand jury
Perpetrator's Age: Unknown
Gender: Unknown
Length of Employment: Unknown

The subject forged two counter-savings withdrawals. One was stamped with another teller's name but was processed through the subject's fund. A customer entered the bank to have her passport updated with the accumulated interest. However, it was found that a large withdrawal had not been marked in the passbook. The customer then filed an affidavit of forgery, and a protracted investigation ensued.

The tellers did not secure their teller stamps. Although this would not have prevented the incident, the lack of security complicated the solution.

This case was remanded to the FBI and was bound over to the grand jury.

Industry: Financial
Type: Fraudulent purchase of third-party installment sale paper
Amount: $12,000
Legal Action: Terminated
Perpetrator's Age: 41
Gender: Male
Length of Employment: 23 years

A respected and trusted employee of 20 years was a leading salesman for a lending company. He ran into financial difficulty as a result of paying his son's college tuition/expenses and his daughter's wedding. He began gambling in hopes of solving his financial dilemma. His manager and other employees were unaware of the financial stress he was under. They knew he gambled occasionally, but they did not realize he was gambling large amounts. He requested a profit-sharing withdrawal and was properly informed that the funds could not be released until retirement or termination.

The employee had check-signing authority to purchase indirect third-party installment-sale paper in the field. The company had long recognized the risk associated with this practice but considered it a necessary aspect of business and had procedural controls over the distribution and accounting for checks used and unused. The employee abused his authority by issuing three checks payable to legitimate distributors, endorsing them, and depositing them in his bank account. He reported the checks on his manual report as void. The first check was written in May; and two more checks were written in November, totaling $10,000.

Existing controls failed when his manager did not properly review the manual reports and physically account for voided checks. The manager did not require that the reports be submitted promptly for his review and approval. The perpetration was detected as a result of notices sent to the manager from the bank-reconciliation department on items paid which were not recorded. The memo included a front-and-back photocopy of the checks.

A notice was sent in August on the first check, but the manager did not recall receiving it. Upon receipt of a second notice on the May item in December, he promptly began an investigation. However, he did not suspect defalcation and was researching reasonable ways in which the reconciling item could have occurred. In January, he received another notice on the two November items. This led him to suspect fraud because of the check endorsement which was more obviously suspicious than the first checks. The perpetrator voluntarily explained what he had done when presented with the bank reconciliation memo and expressed apparent relief that the ordeal was over.

The manager promptly advised top management in accordance with the company's defalcation policy. The internal auditors conducted a complete investigation and found no other evidence of defalcation. The employee was terminated. He signed a promissory note for the $10,000 due upon date of his profit-sharing distribution. He was not prosecuted.

As a result of this incident, the bank reconciliation strengthened its monitoring and reporting controls. A memo was sent to managers reminding them of their duties and responsibilities in properly administering the controls over salesmen checks.

Industry:	Financial
Type:	Improper use of official bank checks
Amount:	$28,400
Legal Action:	Terminated; grand jury returned a "no bill" or not guilty
Perpetrator's Age:	36
Gender:	Male
Length of Employment:	10 years

The fraud involved the manager of a branch office. As an officer of the bank, he was authorized to issue and sign official bank checks. He issued checks without receiving a supporting payment for their purchase. They were drawn payable to friends and family and either deposited to the employee's bank account or used to purchase other official checks. Checks used to purchase other checks were drawn payable to the bank. This procedure involved lapping a check with the register copy of a different check.

The fraud went undetected because of a conversion to a new official check-processing and reconciliation system which was never properly reviewed by operating personnel. Paid official checks were left unreconciled for extended periods of time. A new procedure of review has since been instituted. All unreconciled items are reported to audit and bank security on a weekly basis for review and follow-up investigation.

Industry: Financial
Type: Kiting and diversion of bank funds
Amount: $2,795.86
Legal Action: Charges filed, trial pending
Perpetrator's Age: Unknown
Gender: Unknown
Length of Employment: 6 months

The head teller had access to bank funds and official checks. As a result of personal financial difficulties, he purchased two official checks by using three personal checks drawn on another bank. The official checks were "purchased" in May, 1982. However, the personal checks and credit copies of the official checks were withheld from processing for a week. The teller needed cash and borrowed $800 from his drawer.

As the official checks were paid on May 5, two days before their purchase, they appeared on the "Paid-No-Issue" report. Research revealed the purchaser. When confronted, the perpetrator admitted the action and said he had borrowed the $800 with full intention of returning the money. He claimed there was nothing wrong with the first action but agreed that the latter was against bank policy.

Charges have been filed, and a trial is pending.

Industry: Financial
Type: Lapping customer deposits
Amount: $4,400
Legal Action: Terminated, prosecuted, suspended sentence
Perpetrator's Age: 30
Gender: Female
Length of Employment: 2 years

The teller began shorting her cash fund for minor amounts. Because internal "surprise" cash counts were predictable, shortages were covered prior to audits. Shortage amounts increased and could not be covered. Due to poor cash-audit control procedures, the teller transferred cash which was verified into unverified cash to cover the shortage. Since this was a risky way to cover the ever-increasing shortage, the teller would not deposit checks to customer accounts on the day of deposit. The checks would serve as cash out to cover the cash-fund shortage. The customer's deposit was covered with another person's deposit made a few days later.

The shortage was detected when the teller was required to take a vacation. Since she did not want to delay for a week the processing of a deposit, she cashed a check on a large inactive balance account. The owner of the account complained upon receiving the bank statement.

Industry:	Financial
Type:	Lapping of tax payments, misuse of customer trust allowing complete control over bank account
Amount:	$125,000
Legal Action:	Terminated, prosecuted, sentenced to 6 months
Perpetrator's age:	35
Gender:	Male
Length of Employment:	15 years

The employee served as an assistant branch manager when he initiated the fraud but was later promoted to branch manager. He believed he was underpaid. For several years, he was lapping customers' federal tax payments. As the embezzlement grew larger, he lapped significant sums in the employee-tax withholding of the community in which the branch was located.

The IRS sends delinquent notices to taxpayers when their periodic payments become past-due except in the case of public agencies in which case they inform the collecting bank. This government procedure never brought the problem to light. The manager merely paid the delinquency, which may have been a year past due, and continued to lap current payments. He handled these transactions in a clerical capacity because the bank's personnel department disagreed with audit recommendations that duties should be separated. Finally, management did follow audit recommendations and cut off this avenue to the perpetrator. At this point, he rolled over the embezzlement to a customer's account over which he had complete access, unknown to anyone in the bank.

The customer had great faith in the employee and allowed him to do bookkeeping and checking account reconciliation. The account was substantial, and the fraud ran up to $100,000 before it was stopped. It was caught by a combination of a mysterious entry in the manager's personal checking account and a mistake in the customer's checking account in which a large erroneous charge to that account caused an overdraft.

Industry: Financial
Type: Lapping, use of interoffice account
Amount: $23,000
Legal Action: Terminated, prosecuted, suspended sentence
Perpetrator's Age: 31
Gender: Female
Length of Employment: 4 years

Defalcations consisted of a teller's lapping deposits for certain corporate customers. First evidence was the customer inquiry as to deposits being credited a day late per review of their DDA statement and correspondence with the corporate office. The teller embezzled approximately $10,000 by using an interbranch ticket and claimed to have walked these funds to the vault, although the vault teller never received them. Collusion was not involved.

Industry: Financial
Type: Stealing a government check
Amount: $744.10
Legal Action: Unknown
Perpetrator's Age: Unknown
Gender: Unknown
Length of Employment: 6 months

At an area bank, one proof operator processed all cashed checks. One day when he was processing checks, he came across a government check for which he had authority to cosign. He removed it from the batch and finished the processing. The check was later removed from the bank and destroyed.

When the batch was run through a processing center, it was out of balance. The bank was notified that the item was missing. Bank management recognized the amount as that of the check the operator had cosigned. Confronted with the situation, the subject admitted his crime.

Industry: Financial
Type: Stealing and altering a bank money order
Amount: $25
Legal action: Unknown
Perpetrator's Age: Unknown
Gender: Unknown
Length of Employment: Unknown

A mail opener intercepted a payment with a bank money order. He altered the payee and erased the signer's name, substituting his own.

When the bank money order was returned as "Paid over Forged Drawer" and when the subject was confronted with the item, he admitted only to signing and purchasing the money order. Even when the original maker presented a signed affidavit, the subject continued to deny stealing and altering the item.

Industry: Financial
Type: Stealing from customer deposits
Amount: $4,380
Legal Action: Unknown
Perpetrator's Age: Unknown
Gender: Unknown
Length of Employment: Unknown

The main vault handles cash from other banking offices and deposits from high transaction customers. In such an environment, deposit shortages of $100 or more are commonplace. Therefore, it was simple for a teller to pocket cash and report a customer's deposit as short.

However, when John, a 17-year-old minor, consistently processed short deposits, customers complained; and the bank initiated an investigation. During this period, another teller – Jan – had a deposit which was short over $2,000! The investigators decided to polygraph each employee in the department. The result? Fifteen employees had taken money, nine of which involved more than $5. Six persons were terminated, and one was charged with grand theft.

Industry: Financial
Type: Theft of teller funds
Amount: $937
Legal Action: Terminated
Perpetrator's Age: Unknown
Gender: Female
Length of Employment: Unknown

A teller balanced her cash fund and secured it in the vault, apparently forgetting to remove the loose money from her drawer. Because of miscommunication, management did not check the teller's station at day's end. Sometime between balancing on Friday and Monday morning, the unstrapped monies were stolen.

In preparing the fund for the day's business, the teller noticed that the unstrapped money was missing. An audit of the fund confirmed her suspicion. The teller was terminated for poor performance history.

Industry: Financial
Type: Stolen checks cashed on valid accounts
Amount: $17,000
Legal Action: Terminated, not prosecuted.
Perpetrator's Age: 26
Gender: Female
Length of Employment: 6 years

The perpetrator obtained customer-account balances, numbers, names/addresses, and confidential security codes. The information was then passed to an outside check-cashing ring together with photocopies of signature cards. Stolen checks were then cashed against the account.

The perpetrator supplied outside ring with information and blank temporary account cards which allowed them to go to a branch and make unauthorized withdrawals.

During the investigation, additional procedures were established to require photo/signature identification in addition to the temporary account cards. These procedures curtailed the fraud.

Industry: Financial
Type: Submission of fraudulent items to increase bonus
Amount: $1,500
Legal Action: Terminated but not prosecuted
Perpetrator's Age: 25
Gender: Male
Length of Employment: 5 years

A bank officer, along with numerous other branch-managerial personnel and loan generators, participanted in a program to generate deposits for the bank. An incentive bonus was awarded monthly for each account opened in which the officer had some involvement in encouraging the customer to open the account.

Participants submitted a monthly list of new accounts for which they took credit. The lists were sent to a central location where, without verification, incentives were calculated and paid based on the information submitted.

The perpetrator listed numerous accounts of which he had no involvement. He obtained the names from new account information in the branch where he was assigned.

A fellow employee tipped off an internal auditor when an audit was being conducted. Contact with new account customers quickly revealed the scam. Subsequent confirmations further substantiated the basis for customers' account openings.

Industry: Financial
Type: Submission of fraudulent invoices for payment
Amount: $231,013.
Legal Action: Terminated, prosecution pending
Perpetrator's Age: 35
Gender: Male
Length of Employment: 11 years

While conducting an unrelated special investigation in the property-management division, audit department investigators examined employee checking accounts. One individual's account disclosed several large deposits which were traced to checks drawn on a company's account with another bank. The investigators located 24 invoices paid to this company for work performed totaling $231,031. Further examination of the alleged work performed disclosed that 23 of the 24 were completely fraudulent and that the last was grossly overpriced. All of the invoices had been approved for payment by the suspected employee.

The employee had been with the bank for 11 years and had attained officer status with commensurate responsibility. He appeared competent and was always available for extra hours and emergency work. He was in sole charge of an entire office building's maintenance and had the authority to prepare work orders and to give primary approval for payment of invoices.

When confronted with the audit findings, he admitted he had set up a bogus company and opened the checking account. He had prepared bogus work orders and submitted fraudulent invoices which he approved for payment. Because of his trusted status, the invoices were summarily approved by higher authority without question. The expense checks were deposited to the company's account, and the funds were withdrawn by the employee despite his confession. He never satisfactorily disclosed what had been done with the money. Federal prosecution is pending.

                    Industry: Financial
                        Type: Substituting and holding checks for
                              cash embezzled
                      Amount: $750
                Legal Action: Terminated, not prosecuted
            Perpetrator's Age: 30
                      Gender: Female
        Length of Employment: 3 years

The fraud took place shortly after Christmas and year-end. The employee noticed that all the tellers had been counted by the external audit firm. She had overextended herself during the Christmas season and needed to cover some insufficient checks. She held her own checks, relatives' checks, and another employee's check in her window. She was caught by a surprise cash count by the branch management.

The teller's cash is counted yearly by the audit firm and regulators – semiannually by the internal audit department and monthly by the branch management. These counts have been instrumental for the detection of this type of fraud.

                    Industry: Financial
                        Type: Theft by deception
                      Amount: $658,614.50
                Legal Action: Case remanded to prosecutor's office
            Perpetrator's Age: Unknown
                      Gender: Unknown
        Length of Employment: 4 years, 4 months

The subject was responsible for many duties, one of which was the approval of the purchasing of forms. The subject took bids from numerous producers and chose one with the requirement that the producer pay the subject a "consulting fee." During this time, the bank paid $1,096,245.70 for the forms purchased of which it is believed that the subject received as much as $135,000.

A routine review of invoices revealed an apparently overpriced product. Research of the pricing followed, and coupled with the increasing evidence of affluence over the subject's salary range, a full-scale investigation resulted. The case was sent to the county prosecutor's office.

Industry: Financial
Type: Theft of cash
Amount: $1,000
Legal Action: Terminated, prosecuted, placed on probation
Perpetrator's Age: 21
Gender: Female
Length of Employment: 9 months

A teller whose job it was to take payments and file notes took $1,000 in cash. The employee had already given notice that she would be leaving on the last working day of the year.

On Christmas Eve, a customer brought in ten $100 bills and paid off a loan. The employee removed the loan note from the file with the cash. On the day after Christmas, the employee called and said she would not be back. Fifteen days later, the customer received a past-due notice on the loan. He brought in a copy of the stamped, paid receipt.

The outstanding notes were found to be out of balance by $1,000. The FBI interviewed the employee, and she acknowledged the theft and said she felt she had been underutilized for her skills.

Industry: Financial
Type: Theft of cash
Amount: $3,600
Legal Action: Terminated
Perpetrator's Age: 20
Gender: Female
Length of Employment: 8 months

The teller thought she had found an easy way to make extra money. When a customer came to the window with cash to buy a personal money order, she took the cash, pocketed it, and threw away the credit portion. She also "borrowed" money orders from other tellers so that any trails back would point to another teller who had issued the money orders according to the branch log.

In addition, the operations department had fallen about four months behind in clearing and reconciling stale items in the money-order account. Once they started clearing items, the fraud surfaced. The teller confessed and made full restitution.

Industry: Financial
Type: Theft of ATM funds
Amount: $13,000
Legal Action: Terminated, prosecuted, sentenced to
1 month in jail, 5 years' probation
Perpetrator's age: 21
Gender: Male
Length of Employment: 2.75 years

The management trainee performed numerous assignments in the branch bank where he was training. Through deliberate effort on his part and carelessness of his co-workers, he was able to obtain both the key and the combination to the double-custody facility which housed currency in the ATM machine. Subject obtained both keys to the night locks allowing after-hours access to the branch. None of these keys or combinations had been assigned to this employee, but he had been asked to assist in the balancing operation on several occasions. He had "borrowed" keys assigned to proper personnel and observed the combination being run by another employee.

The subject entered the branch late one night and opened the ATM machine. He took $13,000 in cash and switched the $5s and $20s to make it appear as though the machine had been loaded incorrectly and paid out the wrong denominations. The subject was unaware of the night alarm which went off at 12:01 a.m. Although the police arrived at 12:06, the subject was not seen; nor was he aware of their presence. It took approximately two days to investigate the ATM shortage and determine it was not caused by improper loading. After reviewing the circumstances including the false-alarm report, the loss was considered an inside job. Numerous interrogations of branch staff and service personnel were made before the management trainee admitted the theft. He failed a polygraph examination given by the FBI approximately three months later.

Full restitution was obtained; the subject was sentenced to a one-month jail term and five years' probation.

Industry: Financial
Type: Theft of teller cash
Amount: $20
Legal action: Charged with petty theft
Perpetrator's Age: Unknown
Gender: Unknown
Length of Employment: Unknown

The subject entered teller station to "talk" with a nearby teller. During conversation, the subject removed two $20 bills from the victim's unlocked teller-fund drawer. For reasons unknown, the subject decided to return one of the bills and accidentally dropped it on the floor.

Another teller witnessed this action and reported it to the office's assistant manager. The supervisor had the victim's teller fund audited, supporting the claims of the reporting teller.

Industry: Financial
Type: Theft of teller funds
Amount: $110
Legal Action: Charged with petty theft
Perpetrator's Age: Unknown
Gender: Unknown
Length of Employment: Unknown

A teller put the key to his cash drawer on a counter and then left for approximately ten minutes. While he was gone, the perpetrator entered the teller's station to talk to another employee in an adjoining station. The other teller was busy and didn't watch the subject during the conversation. The subject took the key to the absent employee's teller fund, unlocked it, and took eleven $10 bills.

Upon returning, the victimized teller noticed that the key was not where he had left it, so he counted the teller fund and found that it was short. When he reported the difference, another teller told of seeing the subject in the vicinity of the cage during the time of the disappearance. After an investigation involving numerous interviews, the perpetrator confessed and was charged by local authorities with petty theft.

```
          Industry: Government
              Type: Company payment of personal expenses
            Amount: $2,000
      Legal Action: Terminated
  Perpetrator's Age: 37
            Gender: Male
Length of Employment: 3 years
```

The fraud was committed by an equipment superintendent who had the authority to requisition foods and services plus approve charges or invoices.

Controls consisted of the maintenance-manager supervisor's reviewing charges on a test basis. Also, the accounts payable department matches the purchase order, receiving report, and invoice for payment.

The equipment superintendent passed personal charges invoiced to the company through the control system. The types of charges were the same as what the company normally pays, so the invoices were not questioned by the maintenance manager or accounts payable. Over a period of eight months, the equipment superintendent defrauded the company of $2,000.

An old, outstanding invoice for which the equipment superintendent did not raise a purchase order led to questions, to investigations, and finally to the fraudulent finding.

```
          Industry: Government
              Type: Duplicate death payments, one of
                    which went to perpetrator
            Amount: $14,000
      Legal Action: Terminated, prosecuted, incarcerated
                    for unknown length of time
  Perpetrator's Age: 32
            Gender: Female
Length of Employment: 7 years
```

The retirement system had undergone a major overhaul of its data processing system and related programs. One of the enhancements was the conversion of member-retirement-identification numbers to Social Security numbers.

A major weakness occurring with the conversion was that the computer was programmed to accept both the old employee number and the Social Security number when paying a benefit. Hence, the same individual could be paid twice – once by employee number and second by Social Security number.

During the conversion there was much confusion as some processes changed. Employees, including supervisors, were not fully prepared to operate under the new conditions. Workloads had built up to a point where considerable overtime was being expended.

The perpetrator was "average" with respect to production and learning ability but was considered a poor employee in regards to attendance. The individual was intelligent enough to know of this computer-programming weakness.

The perpetrator was responsible for calculating death benefits. The procedure was to verify the death of the member by reviewing the death certificate, identifying the beneficiary by pulling the member's file, determining the contributions remaining in the member's account by acquiring the data from the computer, applying the standard death-insurance benefit, and preparing an input document for data processing the scheduling of the payment.

The perpetrator prepared one input document to pay the legal beneficiary of record and another to pay herself under a fictitious name. Since the system was operating under a semicrisis mode, no review was made of her work. Also, the computer was not programmed to produce any output or feedback on member payments or the balancing of such accounts, which would have detected an erroneous or fraudulent payment. Consequently, the perpetrator had a handle on the scheme until a bank teller called to verify the appropriateness of a very large check.

Industry:	Government
Type:	Embezzlement of cash receipts
Amount:	$23,930
Legal Action:	Terminated, prosecuted, placed on probation
Perpetrator's Age:	25
Gender:	Female
Length of Employment:	3.5 years

This fraud was made possible by a lack of policies and procedures, a coordination of cash collections, and a transfer of funds between cashiers and accounting department, internal controls, and independent auditors.

The misappropriation of funds was detected through a review of a bank deposit against a collection log kept by the accounting clerk while absent on sick leave. Since the accounting clerk prepared the collection log, daily cash report, and deposits and was able to alter computerized utility individual accounts, she was able to misappropriate a total of $23,930. This was accomplished by preparing daily cash reports that reflected less cash receipts collected than were actually received and depositing the lesser amount in the city's bank account.

The accounting clerk processed the entire accounting transactions. After the discovery of missing funds, she was terminated, prosecuted, pleaded guilty, and was sentenced to ten years' probation.

Industry: Government
Type: Embezzlement of funds transferred between locations
Amount: $28,510
Legal Action: Terminated, prosecuted, placed on probation
Perpetrator's Age: 33
Gender: Female
Length of Employment: 9 years

A nine-year city employee began her career working in the city's accounting department as a cashier and accounts payable clerk and was then transferred to the department of recreation. Her secretarial duties at the new location included billing and collecting rental fees and deposits. She issued some receipts which were not prenumbered. There were no daily cash reports on collections and no report of who transferred the cash collected to the city's cashiers. Consequently, shortages occurred on various transfers.

Further examination revealed that, as she transferred the majority of collections to city cashiers, she verbally specified the breakdown on individual amounts/accounts to be receipted by cashiers. She also prepared and approved deposit refunds to lessors. The accounting department processed check refunds based on general fund-cashier receipts as coded by cashiers. Any complaints on deposit refunds received at the city's accounting department were referred back to the administrative secretary where she would issue direct cash refunds to the lessors.

The city's internal auditor discovered a shortage of funds ($28,510) when conducting a random audit of the department of recreation's cash collections. The department director and administrative secretary were subsequently dismissed after the audit. The secretary was later prosecuted, found guilty, and placed on ten years' probation.

Industry: Educational
Type: Embezzlement of student financial aid funds
Amount: $30,000
Legal action: Terminated, prosecution attempted, perpetrator jumped bail and disappeared
Perpetrator's Age: 29
Gender: Male
Length of Employment: 3 years

The Office of Student Financial Aid (SFA) reported a break-in, and the university internal auditor was assigned to verify the loss of funds in the emergency student-loan collection. Due to the lack of available documentation, the internal auditor was unable to confirm any loss of funds and recommended an audit. During this procedure, the internal auditor found $1,000 (two $500 transactions) that required an additional explanation. All attempts to contact the director failed. His superior, the vice president for student affairs, did not know what to believe. The internal auditor pressured the vice president since the director would not return his phone calls. He even hid out when he tried to catch him in his office. Two months after the investigation began, the director left notes for the vice president stating that he was resigning and leaving town. The director left with his boat and girlfriend.

At this point, the university authorized internal audit to contact the bank about the $1,000. The bank had sufficient documentation to show that the director had received the $1,000 and that it had never been returned to the loan funds. A warrant was issued for the director's arrest. He was found a month later in Pennsylvania and was returned and released on a $25,000 bond. The director jumped bail in 1974 and to date has not been tried for fraud.

Further auditing for other signs of fraud found that the director had aid checks made out to various individuals with inaccurate Social Security numbers. The checks were given to the director for distribution. He deposited the checks into fictitious bank accounts to the tune of about $30,000. The university's insurance policy limited reimbursement to $25,000.

Industry: Government
Type: Embezzling of cash receipts
Amount: $3,089
Legal Action: Terminated, prosecuted,
placed on probation
Perpetrator's Age: 32
Gender: Female
Length of Employment: 3 years

The receipts clerk handled receipts received over the counter and by mail. The perpetrator obtained an out-of-sequence receipt book, receipted cash payments from this book, and converted the cash for her own use. When opening the mail, she took checks and money orders, failed to receipt them to the makers, and wrote receipts to cover the cash taken. She kept a carefully detailed notebook of all monies taken and attempted to deposit all checks within two or three months.

When the fraud was discovered, she had a thick stack of undeposited checks in her pocketbook. The fraud came to light when a payor called the department head to report that several checks issued within two or three months had not cleared the bank. The evidence led to the employee who subsequently confessed.

Industry: Government
Type: Lapping of cash receipts
Amount: $1,191
Legal Action: Terminated, prosecuted,
placed on probation
Perpetrator's Age: 40
Gender: Female
Length of Employment: 5 years

During the internal audit's review of the city's low-income housing project, exceptions to the standard cash-revenue procedures were noted. The city's records indicated that the project had a petty-cash fund of $50. A surprise cash count revealed no cash on hand. In addition, the petty-cash custodian was observed taking something from the petty-cash box and putting it in her clothing when the auditor walked in. A petty-cash-reimbursement request in the amount of $70.58 was found. The custodian was clearly using the funds other than those earmarked for petty-cash expenditures. In this case, it amounted to $20.58 ($70.58 minus $50.00). The comingling of funds is prohibited by city policy. The custodian's action and misuse of petty cash demonstrated that cash-control problems existed at the project.

Internal audit does revenue tests as a standard part of enterprise-fund audits. During the test, it was noted that revenues were not being deposited on a daily basis and that the dates on a number of receipts had been altered. Both actions were in violation of city policies and are typical of a lapping operation. Suspicions aroused, the city's head cashier was notified and alerted to watch for unusual daily cash reports. She noticed some, but they proved to be nonconclusive. It was decided, however, that the lapping suspicions should be followed to a conclusion.

During the reconciliation of receipts to deposits, the petty-cash custodian, who had access to the rent receivable records, cash, and the revenue reports, confessed to lapping funds. It was determined that $1,191 was taken over several months. The petty-cash custodian was fired and prosecuted. Her supervisor, who was responsible for seeing that city procedure for petty cash and segregation of duties are followed, was asked to resign.

Industry:	Government
Type:	Lapping of cash receipts
Amount:	$11,000
Legal Action:	Terminated, prosecuted, placed on probation
Perpetrator's Age:	33
Gender:	Female
Length of Employment:	8 years

The fraud occurred at our senior-citizen-housing facility where monthly rent monies were stolen by the clerk in charge. She covered up the fraud by "lapping" at the end of the month. She reported large amounts of rent money as being "in transit" to the bank at the end of the month. The next month's rent monies were applied on the first couple of days of the month as the previous month's rent. She eventually had stolen an entire month's rent of $11,000 for that facility and could take no more.

She decided to cover up the fraud through a bogus burglary. The police, however, reported that the whole scheme looked suspicious – there was no forced entry, the safe was left open from the preceding night, and the total receipts were gone when they should have been in the bank.

The investigating officer detected lapping through a review of monthly reports. They determined nothing had been stolen in the "burglary" and that the clerk responsible had removed the receipts and falsified records. The clerk pleaded guilty, was discharged by the employer, and has paid back what was stolen as ordered by the court. Her immediate supervisor resigned, as she was aware that the employee was "borrowing" the receipts. New procedures were put into effect; new employees are handling this facility and its rent.

Industry: Government
Type: Submission of false documentation supporting cash disbursements
Amount: $78,540.65
Legal Action: Terminated, prosecuted, sentenced to 5 years
Perpetrator's age: 25
Gender: Female
Length of Employment: 9 months

This fraud was detected by reviewing long-distance calls at the administration department of the library. The sum of $77,369.65 had been misappropriated from the public library by a method of requisitioning payment to vendors and suppliers. The vendors and suppliers, however, received these payments. Unauthorized long-distance telephone calls were charged to the city in the amount of $1,171.

The library-administrative secretary faked invoices, prepared check requisitions payable to the order of ten different vendors of library books and library equipment totaling $77,369.65. These checks were executed at the city finance or accounting department. Some check requisitions were submitted without proper documentation. The administrative secretary picked up the executed checks and then forged the endorsements of the payees. She presented these checks, with the forged endorsements, to the tellers at the city's depository bank where she personally requested that they be cashed in large bills.

It was also found that the administrative secretary was hired at the public library without being properly screened for a previous criminal record. She was on probation for a previous embezzlement when recruited by the city. After being terminated, she was prosecuted, later submitted a guilty plea, and was sentenced to five years.

Industry: Government
Type: Substituting intercepted checks and
money orders for cash
Amount: $7,941
Legal Action: Terminated
Perpetrator's Age: Unknown
Gender: Female
Length of Employment: Unknown

An audit of the court records disclosed an embezzlement of court funds that was perpetrated by the court bookkeeper. She intercepted in-mail checks and money orders before they were receipted, destroyed corresponding traffic dockets, and substituted the intercepted checks and money orders for currency when she prepared the daily deposit.

As a result of these findings, the district attorney investigated the matter and concluded that there was insufficient evidence for criminal prosecution. However, this investigation did result in the bookkeeper's termination. To establish the pattern and potential extent of our losses, the daily court collections between cash and negotiable instruments received for 107 days were analyzed. The breakdown of receipts between the two was compared to the daily bank-deposit slips for agreement. As a result, 154 specific unreceipted checks and money orders totaling $3,680 which were deposited in the place of currency received were found – an average loss of $23.90 per item! By tracing some of the discrepancies to bank-microfilm records, we identified 48 items with specific court cases involving payments of $1,313.

The clerk of the court surveyed traffic case records. The court determined that 537 scattered traffic dockets were missing. The only explanation for the missing records was that they had been removed from court files in connection with the embezzlement. Hence, it was concluded that a significant embezzlement of court funds had transpired.

The court's survey of missing dockets was used to compute the amount taken. Multiplying the 537 missing dockets by $23.90, the average loss per item as determined by our tests, we determined a loss of $12,834.

Industry: Health Care
Type: Diverting patient refunds to personal use
Amount: $40,000
Legal Action: Terminated
Perpetrator's Age: 44
Gender: Male
Length of Employment: 6 years

The atmosphere for the fraud was set by a hospital patient who purchased from two to six health insurance policies. Although unconfirmed, physicians allegedly purchased policies for their patients to make money on the hospitalization.

A business office manager had the authority to obtain the issuer refund checks when a patient's account was overpaid. It was general practice for him to hand deliver the checks to patients. He convinced patients that policies contained "coordination of benefits" and that they were not due a refund because the insurance company did not pay. He would then forge the name of the payee on the back of the check and cash it.

The company was not defrauded; the patients were. However, the manager collected $40,000 over a three-and-a-half-year period. The return of a patient refund to a person who thought no refund was due revealed the fraud. However, the local prosecutor failed to prosecute.

Industry: Health Care
Type: Use of bogus accounts to siphon money from retired employees' accounts
Amount: $17,746
Legal Action: Terminated, prosecuted
Perpetrator's Age: 40
Gender: Female
Length of Employment: 5 years

This embezzlement of funds occurred in a company's credit union. As with most company credit unions, the board of directors, officers, and credit-union office personnel are volunteers from the current ranks of employees and serve in their roles after hours.

In this case, a company junior executive served as chairman of the audit committee with the warehouse manager on the same staff. The purchasing agent served as the credit-union office manager, and a marketing department secretary served as clerk. Several factors allowed the office clerk to embezzle $17,746 over a 20-month period.

The audit committee chairman did not respond to the warehouse manager's concern that some checks written over a five-month period did not "look right." The warehouse manager was quite busy and didn't have time to pursue it on his own.

The office clerk discovered that, if an existing name was slightly misspelled and a new account number which was three higher than an existing number were entered with the misspelled name, it would appear as if it were a secondary savings account to a legitimate one. This allowed 12 bogus accounts to be created into which the balances of three retired employees' saving accounts were transferred, using a seldom used transfer option in the computer. Transaction logs were altered prior to monthly copying/distribution to the credit-union board and officers. Address changes were entered in the computer so that the retired employees' quarterly statements were sent by the service bureau to the company. The clerk typed the correct information on blank statements and sent them to the retired employees. All bogus accounts had the company address and were presumably destroyed on receipt.

The credit-union office manager was required to countersign all the checks, but he did not look at or challenge the supporting authorization document.

The office clerk authorized her own "loan" for an expensive car. Her arrangement included no down payment with monthly installments to repay the loan coming from "series transfers" from the retired employees' accounts, through one or more bogus accounts, into her personal account. To add insult to injury, she selected another option and entered a very low interest rate on her "loan."

This tragic comedy of errors included two annual reviews by the state auditor's office. The records looked good, and most of the faked authorization documentation that supported the statements and G/L accounts also appeared believable and testified to proper internal controls.

All the overriding of controls and account manipulations skillfully done over about 20 months came into focus with the hiring of a perceptive internal auditor. He made several visits to the credit-union office during service hours and discovered an interesting correlative factor to fraud detection: body language. He found that "the eyes are usually registering what is going on in the mind. The emotion that usually registers in a perpetrator's eyes is fright, almost bordering on horror. Look for it! Other tell-tale signs are a twitching mouth, stiffening of the arms and hands, and the overall change of atmosphere when the auditor walks into the office unannounced, especially at the period near the end or just after the scheduled work period."

This case was concluded in the county prosecutor's office shortly after a tearful confrontation of facts in the presence of the company attorney. This first-time offender pleaded guilty, received a suspended sentence, and was placed on five years' probation. The bonding company paid the entire claim, and the clerk settled with the company at 60 cents on the dollar.

Industry: Insurance
Type: Altering policyholder records to generate
a cash-surrender authorization
Amount: $62,000
Legal Action: Terminated
Perpetrator's Age: 62
Gender: Male
Length of Employment: 25 years

The fraud was perpetrated by a life-insurance agent with close to 25 years service whose commission income and market had begun to drop and who needed to make ends meet. He had access to records that indicated policy status on businesses that had no servicing or active agent. He selected policies in which an incorrect address of record was indicated and which had lapsed for nonpayment of premiums to an extended-term status.

The agent then forged the policyholder's signature to a cash-surrender authorization and mailed the form to the home office for processing with instructions that the check be mailed back to him for delivery. After receiving the checks, most of which were in the $200 range, the agent deposited them into his personal bank account by forging the payees' endorsements.

The fraud covered a three-year period and totaled approximately $62,000.

Industry: Insurance
Type: Creating double commissions and duplicate policies
Amount: $10,000
Legal Action: Terminated and prosecuted
Perpetrator's Age: 35
Gender: Male
Length of Employment: 4 years

An agent gave attractive but confusing presentations to policyholders, convincing them to terminate old insurance policies and purchase new ones with the proceeds. The presentations contained totally unrealistic quotes on interest rates and expected dividends.

He had the policyholder complete forms incorrectly and then took a loan on the old policy instead of terminating the contract as had been discussed. Six months later, he terminated the old policy and rolled the proceeds to the new one. This approach circumvented provisions of his contract and created a double commission on the sale of the new policy. The policyholder was not only covered by unwanted duplicate insurance for six months but also lost interest on the money withheld from the new policy and was charged interest on the policy loan. All of these costs were incurred by the policyholder without his knowledge or intent.

So far, 32 cases involving 99 policies have been discovered.

Industry: Insurance
Type: Creating of false loan on policy and cashing check
Amount: $1,638.83
Legal Action: Terminated
Perpetrator's Age: 36
Gender: Male
Length of Employment: 11 years

An agent accepted a check on the pretext of delivering it to the payee, who was his mother. However, he forged the endorsement, signed his own name as guarantor, and deposited the proceeds into his personal bank account. Because the check was for a loan on a policy that the agent had requested, the payee was not anticipating any payment.

A branch manager became suspicious and followed up the transaction with the policyholder. The agent reimbursed the company for the full amount and was terminated.

Industry: Insurance
Type: Creation of fictitious accidents and submitting claims for the accidents
Amount: $53,000
Legal Action: None; perpetrator making restitution
Perpetrator's Age: 30
Gender: Female
Length of Employment: 5 years

An insurance company agent had draft-signing authority to settle company claims. She created fictitious accidents and charged them against real auto and homeowners' policies. In many cases, the claimants' names were fictitious; other times, she forged their names and countersigned the forms.

The fraud was detected when she failed to respond to company interrogations concerning claim documentation. In an audit, the internal auditors contacted approximately 50 claimants and insureds regarding their losses. Based on the responses from these individuals, it was apparent they never received settlement drafts. The agent admitted the theft and began restitution with a 10 percent carrying charge.

Industry: Insurance
Type: Double reimbursement for travel expenses, submission of false expenses
Amount: $75,000
Legal Action: Terminated, prosecuted, suspended sentence
Perpetrator's Age: 40
Gender: Male
Length of Employment: 3 to 4 years

A small subsidiary was located on a foreign island some distance from the parent company. Its operations and accounting procedures were not strictly supervised with the primary controls being budgetary review and limited senior management interaction.

Two officers of the subsidiary used their position to misuse company assets via double reimbursement of travel and personal expenses, use of company funds to purchase personal articles and assets, and reimbursement of some false travel/entertainment expenses. The officers either stole or "used" funds of third-party customers and diverted service business and some related commissions/fees to their privately owned operations.

Industry: Insurance
Type: Failure to charge a fellow employee for an insurance policy increase
Amount: $286
Legal Action: Terminated
Perpetrator's Age: 21
Gender: Female
Length of Employment: 2 years

Two very close friends worked together in the computer-input section of a processing department. One of the clerks who had an employee-auto insurance policy had a chargeable accident. When the authorized documentation from the claims and underwriting departments was sent to computer input for entry, it was given to the friend with a charge for an additional premium. The friends agreed to only enter the transaction on the motor-vehicle-record-history file, which took care of the back-end accounting of the item. They decided not to enter it on the rating file which generated endorsement premiums.

The clerks were eventually caught when the employee added a pickup truck to her policy and complained about the amount of the premium increase. While reviewing the complaint, an underwriter noticed that she had never been charged for her accident. Further investigation led to a confession from both employees.

Industry: Insurance
Type: Filing false medical claims, cashing checks for personal use
Amount: $8,000
Legal Action: Terminated, prosecuted, sentenced to 3 years
Perpetrator's Age: 30
Gender: Female
Length of Employment: 7 months

The insurance claim department had a backlog of claims to be paid, so they hired six temporary employees from a temporary service bureau. The employees were experienced, so minimum training was required. The "temps" were given authority to pay claims up to $2,000 and turned loose to work out the backlog. Payments were processed via the home office computer, which contained employer plans, eligibility for coverage, and claim history. The perpetrator used computer information as to eligible employers and employees. Fictitious claim input was entered into the terminal for nonexistent dependents. Claim checks were issued at the home office payable to a fictitious doctor; the perpetrator used her maiden name as the physician's name. Claim procedures allowed for checks to be returned to the claim processor if requested so that letters could be attached to the check when needed. The perpetrator was able to get the checks and deposit them in her own bank account. In one instance a check was mailed from the home office, but the mailing address had been entered on the terminal by the examiner; this was her own address. Claim files contained no supporting documents for the claim payments, but there was no review of these files by superiors.

After an initial complaint was lodged, the auditors examined cancelled checks and located seven additional fictitious claim payments. The auditor interviewed employers and employees and secured affidavits that claims were not paid on their behalf. The county prosecutor was notified, and the perpetrator was arrested and sentenced to three years in prison. The prosecutor also subpoenaed bank records and discovered that she had deposited claim checks from three other insurance companies where she had also worked. There was also an open warrant for her arrest.

At the time of discovery, the perpetrator had already been released from her temporary employment because the claim backlog had been worked out. The temporary bureau made full restitution to the company.

Industry: Insurance
Type: Filing fraudulent claims
Amount: $130,000
Legal Action: Terminated, prosecution pending
Perpetrator's Age: 26
Gender: Female
Length of Employment: 3 years

A client questioned adverse claim experience that was causing her insurance premium to rise. Initial study by management turned up a falsified claim. The audit department researched all claims processed against the policy and discovered that a claim examiner and an employee of the policyholder were working together to embezzle $130,000 in funds. Further investigation involving auditors and post-office officials revealed that the involved employee was being blackmailed by the claim examiner. With the cooperation of the blackmailed employee, the claim examiner was prosecuted for mail fraud, wire fraud, embezzlement, blackmail, and threatening bodily injury.

<pre>
          Industry: Insurance
              Type: Filing false claims
            Amount: $12,000
      Legal Action: Terminated
  Perpetrator's Age: 25 to 30
            Gender: Female
Length of Employment: 2 to 5 years
</pre>

An insurance company detected altered personal claim submissions from a claim examiner in one of its field offices. In checking this examiner's employee records, they noted she was referred by another employee. They followed this route back through nine current examiners, reviewing all accident and health-claim submissions. They discovered that five of the nine were falsifying data. A complete audit of the location was then conducted, but no further violations were found.

<pre>
          Industry: Insurance
              Type: Filing fraudulent insurance claims
            Amount: $75,000
      Legal Action: Terminated, paying restitution and
                     interest in exchange for sentence
  Perpetrator's Age: 27
            Gender: Female
Length of Employment: 5 years
</pre>

A claims adjuster noticed that it was easy to file claims on scheduled (insured) jewelry. She had an engagement ring appraised at $12,000 and then had it insured with a competing insurance carrier. A few months later, she hid the ring and reported it lost or stolen. She collected on the loss and asked work peers to take out policies and file claims on the ring for a cut in the settlement. They did so, but none of the individuals "victimized" their own employer.

In the meantime, the perpetrator's husband incurred several thousand dollars in expenses restoring a collector's car. The couple had overextended, and the husband balked at the repair cost. He arranged to have bombs thrown into eight cars, including his, on the restorer's lot. The wife's employer (the insurance company) paid for his car. While investigating the claim, a jealous co-worker who was aware of the perpetrator's activities reported that she was running a jewelry fraud on insurance carriers. The investigations solicited a confession from those involved.

Industry: Insurance
Type: Filing of false claims by agent
Amount: $95,000
Legal Action: Terminated, prosecuted, placed on probation
Perpetrator's Age: 50
Gender: Male
Length of Employment: Unknown

An insurance agent with draft authority decided to file fraudulent claims. He colluded with three or four other parties in padding the value of claims and also used his own policy to file a fraudulent claim. Auditing reviewed some drafts and found one which he had written to himself for his own loss. This triggered an investigation, and fraudulent claims amounting to $95,000 were discovered.

He was prosecuted, sentenced, and placed on probation pending restitution. The money gained was reportedly used to buy horses.

Industry: Insurance.
Type: Forged applications for loan
Amount: $12,811
Legal Action: Terminated, prosecuted, incarcerated for 30 days
Perpetrator's Age: 43
Gender: Female
Length of Employment: 10 years

An insurance supervisor was pressed for cash by contractors who were fixing her home. She forged applications for loans on various insurance policies; and when the checks arrived in the branch office she secured them, forged the endorsement, signed as guarantor, and deposited them into her personal bank account. She did not know how the office controls worked and selected policies with "lost" owners, thinking that no one would be able to react to a loan arising on the record. Actually, these policies were carefully controlled. The fraud was discovered, even though the perpetrator temporarily remained unknown. While the investigation continued, her bank notified the insurance company that she had deposited several of its checks to her personal account and also confirmed that at least one of the payees of those checks had not signed it. The supervisor was then apprehended.

Industry: Insurance
Type: Forged applications for policy surrender
Amount: $0 (caught on first attempt)
Legal Action: Terminated
Perpetrator's Age: 28
Gender: Male
Length of Employment: 7 years

An agent attempted to obtain checks payable to the policyholder by forging applications for policy surrender. He intended to forge the policyholders' signatures on the checks and convert the money to his own bank account.

However, when he presented three forms at the same time purportedly signed by different policyholders, an alert clerk recognized an obvious similarity in the signatures and notified internal audit. Internal audit verified that the forms had not been signed by the policyholders.

Industry: Insurance
Type: Forged policyholders' payments to company
Amount: $1,190.40
Legal Action: Terminated
Perpetrator's Age: 56
Gender: Male
Length of Employment: 10.5 years

On three occasions, an agent accepted money which was to be submitted to the insurance company for payment of premiums. He issued personal receipts for the cash but failed to remit the money. When policyholders received their next annual statement showing the unpaid premiums, they contacted the head office.

The agent was a known alcoholic. Although several attempts had been made by the company to help him control his problem, they were obviously unsuccessful because the fraud took place during a period of heavy drinking.

Industry: Insurance
Type: Fraudulent issuance of drafts
Amount: $73,000
Legal Action: Terminated, prosecuted,
suspended sentence
Perpetrator's Age: 24
Gender: Female
Length of Employment: 3.5 years

An insurance company's New York office reported four premium drafts missing. The four were eventually located, but the investigating auditor noted that large numbers of other drafts were cashed at a particular convenience store.

Another auditor was sent to New York to begin a new investigation and learned that an accounting clerk had issued over 170 drafts to various names – some real, some fictitious, and some dead. With a few exceptions, all drafts had been cashed by the clerk and an accomplice at the convenience store for a total of $35,000.

In addition, this same clerk had "sold" the four missing drafts to a salesman in a Manhattan bar who had access to his employer's bank account. He processed the drafts through his employer's account, took $37,000, and fled. He was never apprehended.

Industry: Insurance
Type: Fraudulent use of sight drafts
Amount: $1,500
Legal Action: Terminated, prosecuted, given
suspended sentence
Perpetrator's Age: 30
Gender: Female
Length of Employment: 4 months

An employee who worked in the underwriting department had easy access to sight drafts and completed checks. She made the drafts payable to either her sister or husband and had these people cash them. Normally, sight drafts are used to pay doctors for medical expenses and are limited to $100. If the employee had not become greedy and made them for amounts greater than $100, she probably would not have been caught so quickly.

She also requested that compensation checks be made out to physicians or clinics and then added either her sister's or husband's name to the check so they could be cashed.

Industry: Insurance
Type: Illegal manipulation of policy and pension funds
Amount: $770,000
Legal Action: Terminated, prosecuted, incarcerated for 10 years
Perpetrator's Age: 45
Gender: Male
Length of Employment: 18 years

The company markets products through general agents. Policyholders are considered clients of the general agent, and all communication flows through a general agent (GA). The GA in question represented the company in several counties of a midwestern state by selling pension plans and group life and health insurance. The fraud involved both products.

Through long-time association with the clients, the GA convinced some of them that he could invest pension funds better than the company. He established a separate corporation and issued stock certificates. In some instances, other clients were never advised that funds were not being forwarded to the company. Annual fund-balance statements from the company were mailed to the GA for delivery and were altered to reflect total funds and fictitious earnings. ERISA reports were also altered. Simultaneous to the time of the surprise audit at the GA office, confirmation letters were sent to pension depositors directly. Twenty-two responses indicated discrepancies in the deposits reported as received by the company. During the audit at the GA's office, he was secretive about activities and reluctantly provided copies of bank deposit slips. These were altered in all cases with the explanation that the GA also did factoring and that the funds were coming. The factoring income was blacked out on the slips. The deposit slip totals were listed during the audit. The GA attempted to contact his accountant who had all financial records. But the accountant was unavailable, so the audit was concluded.

Auditor suspicions were communicated to senior financial and marketing officers. The GA was then summoned to appear at the home office to discuss the problem. The responses to the audit confirmations were not yet received at the time of the meeting with the GA. Management was led to believe by the GA that problems were in communication and lack of understanding by the auditor. At the close of the meeting, the auditor informed the GA that the audit would be completed the next day. The GA was alarmed and asked if the audit could be scheduled in two weeks. The auditor rejected the GA's appeal and returned to the GA's office the next day. The accounting records were still not available from the GA's accountant, but the GA again provided the bank deposit slips. These slips did not agree with the copies previously listed. The auditor questioned the GA's employees concerning operating procedures. These people were: receptionist/secretary (daughter), salesman (son), office manager (sister), pension specialist (suspected mistress), and disbursing clerk (family babysitter). None of these persons was cooperative or willing to answer questions.

The auditor left the GA's office and contacted the former office manager. This person was interviewed for a half day and opened a Pandora's Box. He explained in detail the GA's operation not only in the mishandling of pension funds but also describing a scheme for the group life and health business. This involved the GA holding insurance premiums and paying minor claims, thereby becoming an illegal insurance company. When large claims were filed by policyholders, the GA would remit the back premiums to the company, claiming administrative error caused failure to remit on a timely basis. This explanation was accepted by the company, and policies were reinstated at the request of this long-time, good-producing GA. Shortly thereafter, the GA would submit the large policyholder claim for payment by the company. The former employee indicated that the GA had been using this scheme along with the diversion of pension funds for five years. The auditor also received notice by phone from the home office that several confirmation responses indicated deposit discrepancies and that the legal department had received a suit concerning nonpayment of several hospital claims for employees of a tavern which the company had no record of as a policyholder.

The auditor visited each of the parties. The pension depositors provided copies of checks and annual reports. The checks payable to the company were negotiated by the GA. The annual reports were compared to company prepared reports; they disagreed. The tavern owners produced copies of enrollment cards and hospital I.D. cards which were official company forms. The tavern owners believed that their employees were insured by the company. The auditor contacted the county prosecutor and the state insurance office. The prosecutor advised that the GA was under investigation by the IRS, FBI, and the state police for suspected illegal activities in areas other than insurance. The state insurance office advised that the GA was under investigation for irregularities with other insurance companies. The auditor confronted the GA with the specific findings. The GA called his attorney and was advised not to answer any questions.

The auditor returned to the home office and requested immediate cancellation of the GA's contract and formal notice to the state insurance department. A task force was established to research the status of all business written by the GA. All questionable items (e.g., lapsed policies, reinstated policies, delinquent premiums, cessation of pension deposits, law suits, confirmation responses) were investigated. Every policyholder was visited, and copies of checks and any other documents were obtained when it appeared there was some manipulation by the GA. During the investigation, several policyholders brought suit against the GA in federal district court, naming the insurance company a third-party defendant. In all, 34 policyholders had shortages in either pension funds or premium payments. The company made each loss good, which in the aggregate totalled $766,000. The bonding company paid $200,000 of this amount.

The GA was indicted and convicted on 32 counts of embezzling and concealing information and was sentenced to five years in prison. He was ordered to make resitution for funds embezzled, pay a $10,000 fine, and serve five years' probation. The state insurance department cancelled the GA's license for three years and assessed him a $12,000 fine. The GA presently serves in a federal penitentiary. He has not paid the fines as ordered by the court nor has any restitution been made. What happened to the $766,000 has never been determined.

Industry: Insurance
Type: Initiating fraudulent check request,
forging signature
Amount: $5,200
Legal Action: Terminated
Perpetrator's Age: 42
Gender: Male
Length of Employment: 13 years

An accounting supervisor initiated a check request and forged the appropriate approvals, charging a suspense account where unidentified premiums were held. He then notified the person receiving prepared checks that the payee (a fictitious name) was personally coming in to pick up the check. He endorsed the check over to himself by affixing the payee's signature and thus obtained the check. He took the check to the bank and requested $5,000 in traveler's checks and the balance of $200 in cash.

A new teller waited on him. He received $5,000 in traveler's checks, but the teller had to have a supervisor's authorization to pay the $200 in cash. The supervisor noticed that the suspect appeared nervous and decided to call the company. Fortunately, the supervisor made a xerox copy of the check (front and back). The suspect panicked, returned the traveler's checks to the teller, and asked for the falsified check back, which he received. He was terminated when he returned to work. Had he deposited the check to his account, he probably would have been successful.

Industry:	Insurance
Type:	Issuance of fraudulent claim checks
Amount:	$207,000
Legal Action:	Terminated, prosecuted, sentenced to 7 years in prison
Perpetrator's Age:	35
Gender:	Female
Length of Employment:	6.5 years

A routine claim-payment review uncovered a suspicious pattern of payments issued by a claim office to four addresses in the area vicinity. Forty payments totalling approximately $200,000 were identified and had been charged against the XYZ account. Further analysis disclosed that four of the payments had been mailed to the residence address of a claim-terminal operator employed in the office who had responsibility for inputting XYZ claim-payment transactions. Three of these checks bore a payee's name consistent with the terminal operator's maiden name. The fourth bore a payee's name consistent with the employee's son by a previous marriage. No claim files supporting any of these payments could be located, and the payees' names and addresses did not match XYZ eligibility records.

This matter was referred to the Internal Investigations Department, and field investigation commenced immediately. The investigation succeeded in tracing the proceeds of the fraudulent checks to the employee. The employee was confronted with the compiled evidence and provided a signed statement of admissions implicating herself and other family members in an embezzlement scheme which had begun approximately two years earlier.

The employee used her position as a terminal operator, along with previous training as a claim processor, to cause the issuance of the fraudulent checks to addresses where she or other family members received mail. She further advised that she chose payees' names which were aliases for herself or other family members.

The perpetrator was fired and the matter was referred to state authorities who arrested her on charges of insurance fraud, computer fraud, and grand theft. The perpetrator was subsequently convicted on all three charges, sentenced to seven years in jail, and ordered to make restitution to the company.

Industry: Insurance
Type: Misappropriation of policyholder funds
Amount: $26,000.
Legal Action: Terminated and prosecuted
Perpetrator's Age: 42
Gender: Male
Length of Employment: 13 years

An agent used three different methods to direct policyholder funds for his own use. First, he collected single premiums with insurance applications payable to himself but converted them for his personal use and failed to submit the applications. This involved two cases for a total of $400.

Next, he convinced policyholders that they should withdraw funds from existing policies (dividends and policy loans). The policyholders endorsed the checks and returned them to him with the agreement that the money would be reinvested with the insurance company in high interest-bearing accounts. This involved 47 cases for a total of $18,500.

Finally, he forged the endorsement of the payee, signed his own name as guarantor, and deposited five checks for $1,013 into his personal bank account.

In every case, the policyholder should have received some documentation from the company.

Industry: Insurance
Type: Misappropriating policyholder payments
Amount: $3,198.47
Legal Action: Terminated and prosecuted
Perpetrator's Age: 37
Gender: Male
Length of Employment: 8 years

An agent accepted 17 payments for $3,198.47 from policyholders and agreed to submit the amounts to the head office. He issued personal receipts for the money and deposited the amounts in a "trust account" but then withdrew it for his personal benefit.

The payments had to reach the head office by March 1 to qualify as an income tax shelter. Although the agent issued checks to meet the deadline, they were returned by the bank as "NSF."

Industry: Insurance
Type: Submission of fictitious supporting documentation for cash disbursements
Amount: $2,000
Legal Action: None
Perpetrator's Age: Unknown
Gender: Male
Length of Employment: Unknown

A disbursement clerk reviewed disbursement requests and documentation and forwarded them to the clerk who was responsible for entering data into the automated checkwriting system. The check was then printed by the computer and returned to disbursements. A verification clerk made sure the check agreed with documentation, mailed it, and sent the documentation to filing.

The disbursement clerk sometimes created fictitious documentation, forged authorized signatures, and submitted documents to the data-entry clerk. When the checks came back from the computer, he was close enough to intercept them and recover the documentation. He then submitted an accounting entry to void the check and reverse the accounting. Once the reversal was complete, he obtained and destroyed the documentation and the request.

Two things helped uncover the fraud. When an accounting clerk was reconciling the bank statements (she was six months behind), the fraudulent checks showed up as reconciling items because they had cleared the bank. The perpetrator, however, had reversed the accounting and voided the checks so that they were not shown as issued and outstanding. Also, accounting had a habit of carrying forward from month-to-month "minor" unlocated differences – in this case, four or five checks totaling about $2,000.

Although the clerk cashed at least one of the checks himself, collusion was clearly involved with certain payees outside the company. There was also an indication of collusion with another disbursement clerk; but polygraph tests, handwriting analyses, and interviews failed to identify accomplices.

The employee quit during the investigation with no knowledge that he was suspected. The company was unable to prosecute because the bank tellers where the checks were cashed were unable to identify the employee.

Industry: Insurance
Type: Stolen checks forged and cashed
Amount: $48,581.09
Legal Action: Terminated and prosecuted
Perpetrator's Age: 25
Gender: Male
Length of Employment: 4 months

A newly hired agent conversed with employees to build a composite picture of check-issue routines. At the beginning of a long weekend, he forced his way through a locked door and filing cabinet to steal checks from supply. He carefully slit the plastic seal, removed checks from a numbered series, and resealed the batch. When he did not appear for work four days later, the police were called to determine whether he had been involved in an accident. When the police located his car at the airport, internal audit was notified. An investigation revealed cashed checks, which were never issued, payable to the agent. He had forged two authorized signatures of company employees on 16 checks totalling $48,581.09. The typing on the checks was of very poor quality and should have raised suspicions.

Industry: Insurance
Type: Submission of fictitious draft stock
Amount: $43,000
Legal Action: Terminated, prosecuted, placed on probation
Perpetrator's Age: 48
Gender: Male
Length of Employment: 22 years

The director of accident and health payments for a nation-wide claim-paying system was the final authority for approving exceptions to standard procedures and had the final control over monitoring draft (check) stock. Over a 12-year period, he took one to three pieces of blank draft stock per month and completed payments to himself ranging from $115 to $690.

Initially, he removed all evidence from the file after a payment was made. Later, as he became more comfortable with the scheme, he left material in corporate files; this led to his detection.

Industry: Insurance
Type: Submission of fraudulent vendor invoices, personal uses of company facilities
Amount: $150,000 +
Legal Action: Terminated
Perpetrator's Age: 34
Gender: Male.
Length of Employment: 7 years

Activities of the company's in-house printing department was a mystery to everyone but the department supervisor, who closed the shop to all but his employees. He kept all records, approved the bills, received shipments, and made all work assignments. Even his superiors were too intimidated to inquire into the operations. There were vague verbal company guidelines that allowed "personal jobs" to be run on the presses if they were done on the employees' own time. For two-and-a-half years the number of "personal jobs" increased.

Also during this period, the overtime hours increased. Most of the time was put in by the supervisor who did not qualify for overtime pay. An increase was also noted in the number of jobs that had to be sent to outside print shops because the department "didn't have time for all the work."

Auditing noticed that during a four-month period, 76 percent of all printing costs went to outside firms. The in-house printshop was considered large enough to handle all the company work, so an investigation was begun. It was found that the printshop supervisor had worked after hours on the company's own presses, printed phony invoices with names of two friends, approved the invoices and sent them for payment, and made the work appear to have come from outside sources. When the invoices were paid, he met one of his friends at the bank to cash the check and gave the accomplice a small fee for the trouble. These payments amounted to about $50,000. When found, the supervisor was fired; however, he was not prosecuted because of the mercy of company executives. He repaid $8,600, which was his "slap on the wrist." The in-house printing department was phased out four months later. As a result, printing costs for the next three years decreased $370,000.

A debriefing was held with top executives, internal auditors, legal staff, and a few others who were contacted during the investigation.

Industry:	Insurance
Type:	Theft of incoming checks arriving in the mail
Amount:	$95,000
Legal Action:	Terminated, prosecution pending
Perpetrator's Age:	22
Gender:	Male
Length of Employment:	3 years

The perpetrator distributed mail to a department of 40 people. Included in the mail were checks originally written by the company that were being returned by policyholders. For example, a policyholder might decide to delay maturity of a policy or change his mind about taking a policy loan.

The perpetrator worked in an enclosed, private area; and on a number of occasions, he stuffed the checks inside a newspaper and then sold them to others outside the organization who deposited them into several accounts in four city banks.

It is believed that the employee received only a small amount of the $95,000.

Industry: Insurance
Type: Unauthorized sale of company assets
Amount: $2,000
Legal Action: Terminated
Perpetrator's Age: 28
Gender: Male
Length of Employment: 3 years.

During an office review of an insurance company's claim branches, an auditor uncovered an improper claim practice. In matching auto salvage files against the salvage register for accuracy, he noted the name of a buyer who had attempted to purchase salvage prior to its being sold at the salvage pool, which was against company policy. The auditor reviewed the file and found that a 1978 Cadillac was sold directly to a salvage yard and was not bid through the salvage pool. There was no written approval in the file to do so, only the adjuster's note to sell the car on a one-time-only basis with verbal authorization. The supervisor who supposedly gave this approval was on vacation at the time. The adjuster, when questioned, admitted he was aware of company policy and that he had not received approval. He was asked to resign, and the company could not prove that any kickbacks had been given.

Industry: Manufacturing
Type: Abuse of expense account, misuse of company accounts
Amount: $5,000
Legal Action: Terminated
Perpetrator's Age: 52
Gender: Male
Length of Employment: 8 years

Corporate headquarters received an anonymous letter alleging abuse of expense reports and misuse of company assets by management at an operating division. Investigation by internal audit found receipts had been altered, personal purchases of goods had been reimbursed as "meal expenses," personal cars had been repaired at company expense, company equipment had been diverted for personal use, and good material had been declared scrap and then purchased at "fire-sale" prices by the individuals involved.

Industry: Manufacturing
Type: Buyer kickbacks
Amount: $30,000
Legal Action: None
Perpetrator's Age: 48
Gender: Male
Length of Employment: 18 months

A buyer awarded significant business to a favored vendor with spotty delivery and quality performance at prices notably higher than previous suppliers' orders. The purchase requests were properly authorized, but significant variance from estimates were not returned for further review.

An expanded review found numerous pricing irregularities through purchase-order modifications which changed quantities, prices, and extra charges without proper approval. All modifications required approval of the purchasing manager, but the system was not enforced.

Outside investigators obtained an admission from another vendor that kickbacks were paid to retain business with the company.

Industry: Manufacturing
Type: Cashing company checks with petty-cash stamp, altering internal documents
Amount: $15,316.52
Legal Action: Terminated, indictment dropped
Perpetrator's Age: 30
Gender: Male
Length of Employment: 1 year

A district office manager received a call from a customer reporting that his statement showed him owing for an invoice that had been paid. The manager requested a copy showing both sides of the cancelled check. The backside had the stamped endorsement by the bank used for petty-cash checks. The initials were forged, but it was felt to be an inside job.

The employee, an accounting clerk, was absent from the time he overhead conversation regarding the call and the customer's account. Internal audit was notified, and upon arrival all employees had been summoned for questioning. When the perpetrator was questioned, he said he had needed money and had cashed three checks but claimed to have replaced the money with a cashier's check. He showed a deposit containing an entry for the amount of the three checks.

The incident occurred on a Friday, and the bank in question also housed the parent corporation's account. In this type of situation, a corporate officer is required to be involved; but since the corporate headquarters were in another city, an officer was unable to be in attendance on such short notice. Therefore, the employee was simply released.

The following week, copies of the cashier's checks were requested; but bank microfilm revealed that none existed. Instead, there were four additional checks totaling the amount in question which were not listed on the deposit slip. Upon further plant investigation, it was found that the three invoice-file copies were all missing and that the computer printout showed the respective invoice numbers had been voided.

A quick review found that the perpetrator had the responsibility of making out the daily deposit and preparing the sales orders from the previous day. These transactions were prepared for entry into the computer system that produced customer invoices. A minicomputer was acquired to enter the sales orders and had been installed just previous to the perpetrator's assuming these job duties. Before the minicomputer's installation, all sales orders were sent to the division general office for entry; and numbers were maintained there. When the minicomputer programs were written, they were given the same capabilities as the division general office, which included the ability to void numbers. What the perpetrator had done was to take some cash sales, pocket them, void the sales order in the system, and destroy any related documents. He then sent a customer's check to the bank endorsed with the regular petty-cash stamp. The bank was returning cash in amounts up to $1,900.

The district attorney prosecuted the perpetrator. No arrest was ever made, however, because the bank intervened and repaid the $13,316.52 in checks that it had cashed. As far as it is known, the bank never pursued any legal action against the perpetrator.

Industry: Manufacturing
Type: Clocking in for double shifts
Amount: $40,000
Legal Action: Terminated
Perpetrator's Age: 44
Gender: Male
Length of Employment: 12 years

The fraud involved a bargaining-unit employee who was acting in the capacity of a foreman on a maintenance crew. Guards observing the time-card punching were extremely lax in their duties.

The foreman had a fellow crewman clock him in for the first shift and would then show up for the second, obtain his time card, and clock himself out at the end of that shift. He used this trick in different ways to rotate the turn he actually worked. A very large man, he bullied members of various crews to clock him in and out. An anonymous tip came from a person he had attempted to intimidate.

A major problem was the way time cards were handled. Once employees clocked in, their cards were passed to the appropriate foreman. In this case, however, the perpetrator *was* the foreman.

Industry: Manufacturing
Type: Submission of false invoices
Amount: $40,000
Legal Action: Terminated, prosecuted, sentenced to 2 to 5 years
Perpetrator's Age: 38
Gender: Male
Length of Employment: 2 years

The purchasing agent was also the receiving department supervisor who had an office affair with the accounts payable clerk. A process materials salesman proposed a fraud following a discussion regarding the volume used by the company. The purchasing agent knew that the material usage was significantly short of the standard that had been established when the plant was in a start-up mode.

The salesman established an out-of-state phone number and post-office box, but used a legitimate company name. He provided invoices, bills of lading and copies of freight bills, etc. The purchasing agent prepared receiving reports and told the receiving clerk that he received goods after hours or when the clerk was on an errand. The payment check was computer-generated, signed, and mailed to the post-office box of the salesman who received the payment and split the proceeds with the purchasing agent.

It was suspected that the accounts payable clerk was aware of these transactions because of the missing purchase orders from her files.

Industry: Manufacturing
Type: Creation of dummy supplier, submission of fraudulent invoices
Amount: $75,000
Legal Action: Terminated, prosecuted, trial pending
Perpetrator's Age: 28
Gender: Female
Length of Employment: 7 years

The advertising manager had authority to approve vendor invoices after negotiating a purchase of services. The manager created a "dummy" supplier, complete with post-office box and bank account. Monthly invoices in varying amounts were submitted, approved, and paid. The cost was charged to an "off-the-budget" account used for supplier participation payments to assist in special promotions.

The false vendor was discovered during an advertising audit two years later. A confession was obtained, and the amount taken exceeded $75,000

Industry: Manufacturing
Type: Diversion of company cash to pay personal bills
Amount: $50,000
Legal Action: Terminated, prosecuted, placed on probation
Perpetrator's Age: 40
Gender: Female
Length of Employment: 3 years

A chief accountant in a small company location used his check signing authority to pay personal bills. The bookkeeper asked the chief accountant for assistance when differences occurred. This practice continued three years until the accountant explained one payment as a "foreign bribe." The bookkeeper discussed the situation with the sales manager who advised the general manager. The general manager initiated an investigation which uncovered a loss of $50,000.

Industry: Manufacturing
Type: Division of various assets, time, etc., to personal corporation use
Amount: Unknown
Legal Action: Terminated
Perpetrator's Age: 40 (ringleader of perpetrators)
Gender: Male
Length of Employment: 12 years

The perpetrators were high-level employees of a corporate division that operated independently. The perpetrators included the plant manager, controller, at least two salesmen, plus the former plant manager who had been promoted to corporate headquarters as a divisional supervisor.

The perpetrators set up a competing business which was organized to handle small orders which the division did not accept or could not make money by running. However, as their business grew, they gradually encroached on the division's business.

The fraud allegedly included diversion of management time; diversion of work in process from the division to the perpetrator's business, either through third parties, "seconds," or sales below market prices; use of labor at the perpetrators' business; diversion of manufacturing supplies (on a small scale); and diversion of assets.

In addition, it was learned that the general manager and the former general manager took kickbacks including cash, a boat, and other services from at least two vendors.

Industry: Manufacturing
Type: Embezzlement of cash receipts
Amount: $20,306
Legal Action: Terminated, prosecuted, trial pending
Perpetrator's Age: 45
Gender: Female
Length of Employment: 11 years

On June 7, Ms. C received a phone call from Mr. F, or someone calling in his behalf. The purpose was to confirm that the company had received an insurance payment of $132.12 paid in currency the previous Friday. Mr. F had lost his receipt and expressed concern that he would be unable to prove the payment; he wanted to make sure the company had a valid record.

The forms used to record payments received on deposit day had already been forwarded to the credit department. Ms. C went to the empty cash envelopes for that day and looked for one marked "Mr. F $132.12." She was unsuccessful, so she went to the credit department to check the cash-receipt forms for his name. Fortunately, the forms were in the credit department. She reassured the caller that there was no problem and that he had no need to worry because a record of his payment was filed. However, she had not been able to find an empty cash envelope for Mr. F and decided to further investigate the matter.

The next day when the cash-receipt forms were returned from data entry, she called the employee-benefits department to find out which paid insurance invoices had been sent to them from the cashier department on the Friday and Monday in question. She compared paid invoices to the insurance payments listed on cash receipts and found that four invoices had been stamped paid but were not recorded. This implied that four invoices were erroneously stamped and sent to employee benefits or that the payments actually had been made but were not recorded and deposited. She checked the Tuesday cash-receipt forms to see if they had possibly been entered late but was unable to locate them.

At this point, she informed her supervisor, Mr. H., and asked for permission to obtain copies of all checks deposited on June 7. He agreed, so she called the bank and requested the necessary copies. While waiting for the bank's response, she reconciled checks listed on the bank deposit to payments recorded on the cash-receipts forms and cash envelopes. She discovered the amount of currency received from a sports club was more than what had been recorded on the cash envelope by $264.24. She mentioned this discrepancy to the responsible co-worker and asked if she could determine what had caused this incident.

Ms. C returned to work on Monday and checked back with the co-worker, Ms. G, for a report. The latter said she hadn't found anything that might explain the difference in the deposit. Ms. C confronted her with the severity of the problem and pointed out that only the two of them had worked deposits on the day in question. Ms. G said she was not involved but offered to cover the shortage since the records had been written in her handwriting. She delivered a personal check in the appropriate amount to the company that same morning.

When Ms. C received the requested check copies from the

bank, she noted additional suspicious discrepancies. She showed her supervisor where four insurance payments totalling $330.30 had not been recorded on cash-receipt forms and also where checks received for selling aids were underrecorded by $66.06.

While waiting for his immediate supervisor to return from vacation, Mr. H was approached by Ms. G regarding her job security. She told him she would pay back all shortages found for June 7 but that she could not do so in one lump sum. Mr. H informed her that he was not authorized to make a decision and that it would be turned over to the proper personnel.

An audit was begun with the main objective to accumulate information about the cash shortages. The cashier department personnel were interviewed, and an audit was performed of the accounts shorted on the day in question. All cash receipts were found to have cash shortages for a period ranging from the first of February through the end of June. From these test results, a determination was made about which accounts were experiencing significant shortages. Each was carefully audited to determine the extent of the problem. After an exhaustive review, the problem turned out to be more extensive than originally anticipated, totalling over $20,000.

There was no question that someone in the cashier department was responsible for the cash shortages. Ms. G specifically was responsible for improper recording procedures for those transactions where a wrong amount was posted. In the auditor's opinion, this employee was guilty. Upon his convincing recommendation and the evidence, she was terminated.

Industry:	Manufacturing
Type:	Embezzlement of cash receipts
Amount:	$45,000+
Legal Action:	Terminated
Perpetrator's Age:	Unknown
Gender:	Female
Length of Employment:	8 years

The fraud was a classic example of poor separation of duties between the cash receipts and accounts receivable operations. As the office manager in charge of these operations with the ultimate responsibility for providing an aged-accounts-receivable trial balance to the division office, this person's position allowed her to carry out activities undetected. She even had two clerks in the office who posted the account ledger cards (via data terminal).

They were unaware of what was going on until a clerk attempted to find a missing ledger card when the office manager was out of the office.

This clerk found several different aged-trial balances with different amounts. Not knowing which was right, she brought it to the attention of the general manager. The regional accounting manager was called in to review the situation. After an analysis, he and the general manager summoned the office manager for questioning. She admitted taking some of the company funds and depositing them in her personal checking account. The bank in this case had helped her out, as they never questioned the unusual deposit.

Industry:	Manufacturing
Type:	Embezzlement of cash receipts
Amount:	$37,000
Legal Action:	Terminated, prosecuted, placed on probation
Perpetrator's Age:	55
Gender:	Female
Length of Employment:	15 years

A plant accounting clerk was responsible for accepting payments for employee sales, preparing a triplicate sales ticket/receipt (prenumbered), preparing and making bank deposits, and conducting summary sales reports to area offices. She reported directly to an office supervisor whose responsibilities included reviewing summary reports, accounting for serial numbers, and approving reports and documents.

The perpetrator perceived that the supervisor did not regularly account for the numeric sequence of documents. She would occasionally withhold cash and destroy or hide the office copies of the sales ticket. Over a three-year period, she diverted about $37,000 of funds to her own use.

The fraud was detected when auditors tried to account for the numeric sequence of tickets. The gaps led to a search of the office during which numerous unreported tickets were found in the perpetrator's desk and in various files.

An appeal to plant employees on the pretext of trying to reconstruct destroyed records yielded a large number of sales tickets representing unrecorded sales. The company collected $25,000 from its bonding company on the basis of this evidence.

As to the perpetrator, she clung to her claim of innocence

even though she was tried, found guilty, and given a suspended sentence. The bonding company recovered $330 from her, representing the total of specific charges for which she was convicted.

Industry: Manufacturing
Type: Embezzlement of delinquent accounts payable
Amount: $90,000
Legal Action: Terminated, prosecuted, trial pending
Perpetrator's Age: 35
Gender: Male
Length of Employment: 6 years

The delinquent account collector was the perpetrator of fraud who worked approximately two years before beginning his scam. He embezzled $90,000 from one customer. He collected money during day or night, deposited it, and gave his boss the deposit slip. The customer paid and continued to pay with cash, not check. The collector deposited only part of the collected monies. Statements were not mailed to customers, and bank accounts were not reconciled. This wouldn't have detected it since, in most cases, the deposit equalled the amount recorded.

Too much trust had been placed in the employee, allowing him to continue this practice even though his boss realized controls were poor.

Industry: Manufacturing
Type: Embezzlement of incoming cash and travel advances
Amount: $48,000
Legal Action: Terminated
Perpetrator's Age: 30
Gender: Female
Length of Employment: 4 years

A fraud totalling nearly $48,000 was perpetrated by an accounting supervisor over the course of one-and-a-half years. The supervisor, highly regarded and completely trusted, successfully used two sources – travel-advance system and incoming cash – to misappropriate funds. A host of controls that should have been in place were not operating, allowing the fraud to continue for many months.

Cash advances to employees are routinely analyzed by treasury department's accounts payable section for outstanding amounts in employees' travel accounts. In carrying out this analysis for the accounting supervisor, two questions arose:

Why were some advances outstanding for several months, and why were many advances cleared by "repayment" rather than by means of an approved expense report? The supervisor had, in fact, received advances totalling $15,000 during the preceding year but had submitted expense reports for only about $3,000.

These unorthodox transactions aroused the suspicion that company funds were being used improperly. After a short preliminary investigation, it was established that the employee had falsified records so as to fraudulently remove almost $16,000. He was terminated from service.

A thorough investigation was conducted into other functions that had been under his jurisdiction to determine the extent of the fraud. An additional $32,000 of misappropriations was uncovered, all subsequently acknowledged to have been the result of activities he undertook.

Industry:	Manufacturing
Type:	Embezzlement of petty cash and perpetrator's making duplicate personal paychecks
Amount:	$40,000
Legal Action:	Terminated, prosecuted, trial pending
Perpetrator's Age:	28
Gender:	Female
Length of Employment:	21 months

A small, remote subsidiary was staffed by an inept controller and an accounting clerk who was living beyond her means. The control environment was virtually nonexistent as there were too few employees to allow for proper segregation of duties, and compensating controls such as closer supervisory review were not instituted.

The accounting clerk had cradle-to-grave responsibilities for payroll and cash disbursements. The situation was further aggravated because the site was on a two-year audit cycle, despite known and reported deficiencies. The fraud was perpetrated over an 18-month period beginning four months following an audit. The accounting clerk used blank, voided payroll checks for an extra weekly paycheck. She ran an entire payroll on the computer, voided the run, and pulled out and affixed the signature

141

to her own; she also used the general bank account by drawing and cashing checks made out to "petty cash" from checks annotated in the disbursements ledger as "void" or just not entered (i.e., missing number).

Two of the many changes instituted as a result of disclosures are (1) that small subsidiaries which lack the ability to segregate duties are not allowed to have or use a signature plate and (2) that we visit small activities which are deemed to have a poor control environment at least annually.

Industry:	Manufacturing
Type:	Kickbacks involving the sale of scrap metal
Amount:	$340,000
Legal Action:	Terminated
Perpetrator's Age:	40
Gender:	Male
Length of Employement:	10 years

Company S manufactures and sells wear-resistant alloy parts for commercial applications. The scrap metal generated by the manufacturing process is valuable because of the high cost of the raw materials which include cobalt, tungsten, and chrome. After refining scrap to remove impurities, it is resold to S or others.

However, not all the metal sent by company S to K at company T for cleaning was returned. Part of the proceeds from scrap sales was returned to employees A and B who were acting in collusion with K. To cover up the fraud, A and B falsified invoices and other documents regarding weights and types of metals sent to company T.

While still employed by S Company, A and B misappropriated trade secrets and other confidential information of both a technical and a business nature for use by company C, a business competitor whose outstanding shares were subsequently purchased by A. Employee B also secretly admitted to former employees of S's plant that G had obtained technical know-how for use by C.

Employees A, B, and G had all signed agreements not to disclose confidential information to others gained through their employment with S. Technical knowledge had been accumulated in over 40 years of operations.

After employees A and B resigned , A became an officer and director of company C, which then solicited business from S's existing customers.

The fraud was discovered when a metals dealer, who had also been receiving kickbacks from K but had the arrangement terminated, told S management about the activities of A and B. K was given limited immunity from prosecution in return for his agreement to provide testimony against A and B. He stated that, over a period of several years, he had paid A a minimum of $200,000 and B over $100,000 in kickbacks. Company S then sought, and was granted, an injunction restraining Company C and A, B, and G from using any of the trade secrets or other confidential information improperly obtained.

Company C and former employee A filed for bankruptcy. Former employee G decided to turn against A and B and provided damaging evidence regarding their theft of confidential data from S. Little if any recovery is expected from A or C.

Company S did recover approximately $340,000 from its insurance carrier for losses proven to have resulted from the misappropriation of trade secrets and other acts of unfair competition, breach of contractual and other duties, conversion, and unjust enrichment by A, B, and G.

The fraud was allowed to occur in part because of weaknesses in the internal controls over accounting for scrap by S plus the collusion between A, B, G, and company C. The motivation of A, B, and G appeared to be self-enrichment only.

Industry: Manufacturing
Type: Kickbacks
Amount: $500,000+
Legal Action: Terminated
Perpetrator's Age: 42
Gender: Male
Length of Employment: 15 years

This was a very complex fraud involving two salesmen and customers. During a time when the demand could not be met for products and customers were begging for more, these individuals put the squeeze on for "kickbacks" or shares of stock in companies they supplied.

Additionally, one customer set up a corporation. The salesmen were given 10 percent ownership and sold large quantities of first-grade product to this corporation as a substandard product at a greatly reduced price, involving collusion.

Industry: Manufacturing
Type: Merchandise stolen from loading dock
for resale
Amount: $20,000 (estimated)
Legal Action: Terminated, prosecuted, decision
being appealed, countersuit filed
Perpetrator's Age: 58
Gender: Male.
Length of Employment: 20-plus years

Products produced by the plant were sent to the loading dock for distribution on delivery trucks by using a predetermined loading sheet. The dock supervisor and four delivery men collaborated to obtain extra stock for resale, splitting the profit between them.

Production was "roughly" reconciled to load sheets, but discrepancies were blamed on the producing plant counts or to "unaccounted for" losses. Finally, the differences became so large that a task force was assigned to see if problems could be spotted. One of the drivers confessed prior to the investigation's finish because he knew he would be caught.

Industry: Manufacturing
Type: Overcharging by related party, purchase
of personal items
Amount: $44,000
Legal Action: Terminated
Perpetrator's Age: 42
Gender: Male
Length of Employment: 8 years

A regional manager's wife owned the brokerage firm used to import products into Canada. The brokerage firm handled the payment of import fees and taxes. The firm overcharged on taxes due and kept the difference between them and what was paid to the Canadian government.

Also, all supplies and fixed-asset equipment for the firm were purchased through the regional office. The regional manager took deposits made on products, put them into his personal savings account, and collected interest. In addition, a new heating unit and a snowblower were purchased for the manager's home.

Industry: Manufacturing
Type: Purchases from related parties at overstated price
Amount: $400,000
Legal Action: Terminated
Perpetrator's Age: 45
Gender: Male
Length of Employment: 7 years

The fraud took place in a recently constructed plant for a multiproduct operation (ship, rail, and truck facilities). During one period in the early production phase, the purchasing, receiving, and traffic functions were the responsibility of one man. All three of these functions reported to him.

This employee began buying lime and resold it to the company. He leased his own trucks to do the hauling and authorized these services as head of purchasing. He also shorted weights on lime receipts, coercing employees in the receiving department to falsify tickets and overcharge freight.

After one to two years, the employees complained; and an investigation began. The perpetrator disappeared before court action could begin.

The newness of the organization contributed to improper duty segregation and control. The perpetrator was assigned multiple responsibilities before plant operation expanded when risk was less. Unfortunately, the problem was not corrected in time.

Industry: Manufacturing
Type: Submission of false documentation supporting cash disbursements
Amount: $80,000
Legal Action: Terminated, prosecution in process
Perpetrator's Age: 35
Gender: Female
Length of Employment: 2 years

Sue, the first assistant, made out false receiving documents showing her boyfriend as the vendor. She prepared checks and obtained the necessary signatures.

Joan, a second assistant, worked similar "purchases," using the same method. As office manager, Mary either knew and said nothing or else was extremely naive.

Large purchases went unquestioned by the unit manager who, at times, signed blank checks.

Industry: Manufacturing
Type: Submission of fraudulent check authorization
Amount: $11,750
Legal Action: Terminated, prosecuted, trial pending
Perpetrator's Age: 38
Gender: Female
Length of Employment: 15 years

A 15-year employee working in the controller's function falsely and fraudulently prepared check authorizations totalling $11,750 and $15,998 respectively. The $11,750 check was obtained and deposited in the employee's personal checking account, and the monies were subsequently used for personal expenses.

Existing internal controls were properly followed regarding the $15,998 check. When the employee was confronted with the evidence, she admitted involvement in the improper issuing of checks.

The employee was dismissed for theft of funds and signed an agreement to repay the company. The evidence was turned over to local authorities for prosecution.

Industry: Manufacturing
Type: Submission of false invoices, documents, etc.
Amount: $25,000
Legal Action: Terminated, prosecuted, placed on probation
Perpetrator's Age: 35
Gender: Male
Length of Employment: 13 years

Violation of policy requiring the final phase of a plant closing to be supervised by personnel continuing their employment at other locations was the root of this fraud.

The credit manager was the last office supervisor during the final phaseout. As such, he had access to company checks, control over the bank reconciliations, and originated documents supporting final payments to suppliers, customers, and employees. The loss occurred when false documents triggered checks to certain suppliers, which were intercepted prior to mailing, endorsed by hand, and deposited into a bank account which had been opened in the name of a fictitious company.

Industry: Manufacturing
Type: Submission of fraudulent invoices and covering up payments
Amount: $56,453
Legal Action: Terminated
Perpetrator's Age: 44
Gender: Male
Length of Employment: 14 years

A former office administrator of a branch used his position of responsibility to misappropriate company funds. He embezzled approximately $66,000 from the company over a three-and-a-half-year period.

The employee established an account number in the name of R & S Services at the city bank. Periodically, he typed invoices from R & S numbers and corresponding dollar amounts and stamped them approved. He charged the invoice total to the ECP account on a particular EnVico controls installation job which had sufficient money allocated for purchase of products manufactured by parties other than EnVico. Since the employee was authorized to sign EnVico branch checks up to $500, and later up to $1,000, he would prepare a company check by naming R & S Services as payee in the amount of the invoice. He had the responsibility of preparing a weekly ledger for the branch manager identifying checks to be signed for items purchased that week. He left a blank line on the ledger when submitting it and checks to the branch manager for approval and signature. After it was approved, he would enter the R & S Services check on the ledger, sign the R & S Services check on behalf of EnVico, and deposit the check in his bogus company's account.

Industry: Manufacturing
Type: Submission of time card for ghost employee
Amount: $24,500
Legal Action: Terminated and prosecuted
Perpetrator's Age: Unknown
Gender: Unknown
Length of Employment: Unknown

An industrial relations manager of an outlying plant collected time cards, sent in payroll-order forms, and handled disbursement of payroll checks. He entered a fictitious employee into the system under a direct labor budget and sent in a weekly time card for him over a four-year period. Due to the number of employees hired, this was very difficult to detect.

However, when the company terminated its pension plan, the "ghost" came to life. Previous to this finding, the "new hire" policy had been very slack.

Industry: Manufacturing
Type: Theft of postage
Amount: $14,400
Legal Action: Terminated and prosecuted
Perpetrator's Age: 32
Gender: Female
Length of Employment: 4 years

Postage meter tapes were being run off the postage machine and taken to the post office for refund with no preventative controls.

Postage meter replenishments were in excess of the machine's capacity – request was for $10,000; postage remaining in machine was $700; capacity was $9,999. The post office refunded the difference of $701 to employee in stamps or a money order, which was easily cashed. Receipt for $9,299 placed into the machine was never compared to the original check-request amount.

The perpetrator hired her sister to work for her against company policy. When discovered, termination of both was discussed. Because the supervisor was considered a key employee, only a severely written reprimand was given. Her sister was transferred to another department and later resigned prior to discovery of the fraud.

Industry: Manufacturing
Type: Unauthorized sale of merchandise for cash, falsification of inventory records
Amount: $25,000
Legal action: Terminated
Perpetrator's Age: 30
Gender: Male
Length of Employment: 5 years

The manager of a branch-sales office had complete control of all record keeping reports and files. He also controlled cash receipts and inventory. His supervisor was hospitalized approximately 50 percent of the time.

The fraud began shortly after the manager purchased an expensive home and when he simultaneously suffered a significant drop in income as a result of an unexpected bankruptcy of a large customer. To compensate, he found a customer willing to pay cash for merchandise priced below cost. He arranged to have inventory records falsified by the public warehouse manager where company goods were stored. This activity went on for several months.

When a routine audit was announced, he began scrambling to "fix" records and inventory. He successfully petitioned top management for postponement of the audit . . . to no long-range avail. Within three months, the fraud was discovered by a series of mistakes. The company's loss was about $25,000; almost half was recovered from the insurance company.

Industry:	Manufacturing
Type:	Use of company materials for personal reasons, falsifying hours
Amount:	$125,000
Legal Action:	Terminated
Perpetrator's Age:	45
Gender:	Male
Length of Employment:	6.5 years

The fraud took place in a 50-member maintenance department. It involved the maintenance superintendent and eight other employees including one foreman. Since the members worked on various facilities, they had mobility and were away from the main plant for extended periods. They also transported supplies from one facility to another for use in their projects.

The fraud involved removal of materials and supplies to the maintenance superintendent's house. Some were used for remodeling his home; others were distributed from his house to unknown locations. Some specialized items were ·even ordered through the purchasing department, allegedly for maintenance projects.

Six hourly employees were involved in the fraud by working on remodeling of the superintendent's house while on the clock at the main plant. They were sent out on paperwork given them by their foreman stating that they were going to one of the outlying facilities for a maintenance project. It was suspected that they had an actual contracting company on the side.

Time cards for these employees were falsified to cover their hours away from the company. Fraudulent overtime was also added to increase the amount of the fraud.

The crime came to light because the security manager noticed an unusual amount of "scrap" material being taken from the premises by members of the maintenance crew. Surveillance of maintenance employees took investigators to the superintendent's house. Inspection of time cards disclosed alterations and forgeries. The superintendent, foreman, and seven hourly members were terminated. No criminal prosecution was undertaken. However, a claim was made with the insurance carrier; so possible civil action is pending.

Industry: Manufacturing
Type: Use of fictitious customer to divert cash
Amount: $125,000
Legal Action: Prosecution pending
Perpetrator's Age: 42
Gender: Male
Length of Employment: 10 years

The perpetrator was leaving the company under positive circumstances to become the manager of an independent distributor of the company's products. Unknown to the company, he was already functioning in his new position. He then had his second in command at the company prepare a financial agreement with a fictitious customer of the distributor. The preparer did not question the transaction because of trust in his boss. The perpetrator approved the transaction; the funds were forwarded to the distributor; and he then diverted them for personal use. Before leaving the company, he used knowledge of system weaknesses to remove records of interest due on the note and extended the payment due date. When the note was not paid, the perpetrator was contacted in the new position shown as guarantor of the note. He advised that the debtor was in bankruptcy and that the distributor was repossessing the equipment but needed an extension. The details went unchecked because of trust in the individual, so a second extension was granted. The fraud was detected by internal audit when this transaction appeared in four different tests for conditions of high exposure for fraud.

Industry: Mining
Type: Embezzlement of joint-venture funds
Amount: $4,500,000
Legal Action: Terminated, prosecuted, outcome pending
Perpetrator's Age: 55
Gender: Male
Length of Employment: Not a direct employee

The company participated with several others in mining exploration, which was operated by a promoter who had no economic interest. He was a specialist in this particular kind of mine. After hearing rumors about unusual occurrences at the mine, an audit was begun of the joint-venture expenditures. Major contractors had complained that payments for services were seriously delinquent.

By the time the audit began, the promoter had filed for protection under Chapter 11. Proof of payment was requested in order to verify that billed expenses had actually been paid. When given the bank statements, large wire transfers for funds were noted from the joint-venture accounts to other companies owned by the perpetrator. During the audit, the following was also documented:

1. Most of the 4.5 million advanced by the joint ventures had either been diverted or paid to related party companies for billed services.
2. Purchases from related party companies for major supplies (equipment and tools) had been inflated well above prices charged by other suppliers in the area.
3. Services had been billed by related party companies which appear never to have been provided.
4. Substandard materials had been used and billed at new materials prices. The operator had to replace the mining engineer who refused to allow men in the mine.
5. The mine was shut down without the permission of the other joint venturers.

```
          Industry:  Retail
              Type:  Credit card fraud
            Amount:  $800
      Legal Action:  Terminated, prosecution pending
   Perpetrator's Age:  35
            Gender:  Male
Length of Employment:  3 years
```

The employee was a supervisor in the security department who had two accounts with the company which were in collection status. He used fraudulent information in opening a third account (i.e., different Social Security number, conflicting employment records, and birth dates). He drew attention to himself when the credit manager, after being asked to extend the limit on his account, noticed many discrepancies on his credit application. A subsequent investigation revealed that he was involved in many other credit-card scams totaling $50,000 and involving at least seven other companies.

He was dismissed; prosecution is pending.

```
          Industry:  Retail
              Type:  Kickback
            Amount:  $200,000
      Legal Action:  Terminated, prosecuted,
                       placed on probation
   Perpetrator's Age:  40
            Gender:  Male
Length of Employment:  11 years
```

As is common in this industry, the buyer and the supplier negotiated a unit price for a product with terms that included an optional advertising allowance. They also verbally agreed that, for every unused or unreported dollar not charged to the supplier, the buyer would enjoy a discount.

The buyer eagerly refused to use $800,000 of free corporate advertising in exchange for $200,000 in gifts. The supplier saved $600,000.

Industry: Retail
Type: Kickbacks
Amount: $900,000
Legal Action: None
Perpetrator's Age: 45
Gender: Male
Length of Employment: 7 years

The company decided "distributed processing" was the way to go on inventory. A decision was made to use a certain computer manufacturer for 12 systems. The first system was brought in, and EDP audit was assigned to the project. Problems were encountered with the development. EDP audit reviewed the selection of the system because of (1) nonstandard language and no expertise on the DP staff in that language and (2) incorrect communications protocol which required the processor to handle communications. The audit staff noticed that a major vendor was not included in the bid process and that all vendors included were technically unqualified or only marginally qualified. The auditors began obtaining independent verification of the selection by sending requests for proposal to other qualified vendors with an internal audit return-mail envelope. EDP audit requested sales information as a personal (not company related) request.

The final analysis revealed that the systems selected were overpriced by $20,000 each. Other qualified vendors proposed systems with proper protocol and standard COBOL language at lower prices. EDP audit was contacted by one vendor salesman who was on the team that originally selected the system and who told of the payoff deal made between the company's vice president and his prior company. EDP audit requested and received copies of internal documents that he had.

During the investigation, all systems had been ordered and installed at a cost of over $900,000. Requests from the audit department to delay installation were not honored, and problems that were pointed out were ignored.

The vice president of finance resigned, and a replacement was hired. Verbal reports were given to the new employee about the findings along with reports to the president and to the board of directors.

The auditor left their employ during this transition.

Industry: Retail
Type: Overstatement of expenses from party related to perpetrator
Amount: $310,000
Legal Action: Terminated, prosecuted, placed on probation
Perpetrator's Age: 40
Gender: Male
Length of Employment: 2 years

The perpetrator was responsible for new buildings and construction. He also owned a company (with his family and a friend) that he used to subcontract on company jobs. His personal company billed this company for work at higher prices for labor, materials, etc.

Account payable checks were delivered to him personally at home. It was found that the fraud was spread over a year to include several jobs.

Industry: Retail
Type: Submission of false documentation supporting cash disbursements
Amount: $15,000
Legal Action: Terminated
Perpetrator's Age: 40
Gender: Female
Length of Employment: 8 years

A bookkeeper in a $3,000,000 retail unit had earned a position of trust; so various functions normally reserved for management were assigned to her, including the authority to issue and authorize customer refunds.

However, she issued refunds to nonexistent customers, creating documents with false names and addresses. She adjusted the accounting records and kept the cash.

She was caught when internal audit sent routine confirmations to customers on a mailing list and received excessive "return-to-sender" replies. The following investigation disclosed a telling pattern. The bookkeeper initially denied accusations but admitted the crime upon the presentation of evidence.

Industry: Retail
Type: Submission of fraudulent fees by collection agency for money not collected
Amount: $750,000
Legal Action: Terminated, statute of limitations invoked
Perpetrator's Age: 45
Gender: Male
Length of Employment: 9 years

The credit manager allowed the collection agency, which was attempting to collect on overdue credit-card purchases from customers, to submit fees at 40 percent for monies they never collected.

Employees in the credit department were responsible for matching alleged collections to the cash-receipts book. The credit manager ordered his employees to omit this checking procedure for the agency on the basis that the manager would personally be responsible for them.

Since credit-card volume was increasing dramatically during this period, no one questioned the rise in collection fees. When senior management questioned the high fees to one agent, the credit manager convinced them the agent was just doing a superior job.

Industry: Retail
Type: Submission of fraudulent transactions by payroll manager
Amount: $15,000
Legal Action: Terminated
Perpetrator's Age: 30
Gender: Male
Length of Employment: 5 years

The payroll manager used his broad scope of authority and personal power to have several subordinates process fraudulent transactions based solely on his signature and vague explanations. The payroll manager used several types of transactions, kept the amounts low each time, and used minor but creative techniques to make acts less obvious. Discovery would have been unlikely had he maintained this methodology.

When a conscientious subordinate was first asked to put through an unusual transaction, he did so but became increasingly suspicious. Only through luck, awareness, and discussion with other department employees was internal audit able to unravel the other transactions. The individual, who was terminated by the company, returned the amount discovered out of his pension/termination pay.

The decision criteria for nonprosecution were never made clear. Legal fees and company image were considered. In the end the perpetrator was not prosecuted.

Industry: Retail
Type: Use of fraudulent credit accounts and extending limits on other accounts
Amount: $5,000.
Legal Action: Terminated
Perpetrator's Age: 26
Gender: Female
Length of Employment: 5 years

An employee in a credit department worked in a section which authorizes new accounts and extends the limit on old ones. Her husband applied for credit and was issued a fraudulent account. He went to a travel agency and purchased a roundtrip, direct-flight airline ticket valued at $900. He then cashed in his ticket, received $300, and purchased two indirect tickets costing $600.

The employee also extended the credit limits on accounts belonging to her friends and mother. She was unauthorized to make such adjustments, but she lied to a supervisor to obtain his authorization number. This enabled her to make adjustments.

The series of events which led to her downfall began when a security agent of a branch store identified her as one of three individuals using a newly opened account number which was not entered into the company's system. A subsequent investigation led to her dismissal.

Industry: Service
Type: Collusion involving submission of inflated invoices for services rendered
Amount: $20,000+
Legal Action: Terminated
Perpetrator's Age: 45
Gender: Male
Length of Employment: 5 years

The perpetrator was responsible for obtaining visual aids for use in marketing presentations. In conjunction with various vendors with whom he had a long-time association, inflated bids were submitted; and invoices were paid for amounts far in excess of prices available elsewhere. The perpetrator either received cash from the vendors, had debts paid by them, or was provided with prostitutes.

The audit investigation revealed that the perpetrator had requested similar arrangements from many other vendors who had turned him down. The vendors did not inform the company for fear of being excluded from other work.

The perpetrator reimbursed the company for two instances where no services were received from vendors in return for payments. He was forced to resign.

Industry: Service
Type: Embezzlement of cash from employee fund
Amount: $1,500
Legal Action: Terminated
Perpetrator's Age: 40
Gender: Male
Length of Employment: 5 years

The business unit had a small employee fund which was used for parties, sporting events, barbeques, etc. A checkbook for the fund was maintained in a local bank. The fund's primary source of revenues came from the sale of soft drinks from the cola machines, although additional revenues were generated from the sale of scrap metal, batteries, and drums.

A company informant told the director of internal audit that the fund was being misused. Upon investigation, it was found that the manager was paying for minor automobile repairs from funds rather than report the accidents as well as employee doctor bills for minor injuries. This was done to curtail accident reports which were used as performance measurements. The manager also paid some rather large country-club-entertainment bills from the fund rather than report them, since his superior would be required to review them and determine approval. Finally, he had purchased a riding lawn mower for residential use.

Although the amounts were minor, the offense was considered to be very serious. The manager was immediately terminated, even though he was to be promoted the following day. His response? "Everyone does it!" He was not prosecuted.

Industry: Transportation
Type: Filing fraudulent claims for furniture losses
Amount: $60,000
Legal Action: Terminated, prosecuted, placed on probation
Perpetrator's Age: 30 to 32
Gender: 5 males, 1 female
Length of Employment: 2 years on the average

Four current employees, two former employees, and approximately 20 of their friends and relatives were indicted by a county grand jury on charges of theft and conspiracy involving phony claims.

The theft occurred in the company's claims department where claims adjusters settle with customers for lost or damaged furniture shipments. Adjustment checks not exceeding $750 did not require a supervisor's approval. Some 68 checks ranging from $550 to $750 were paid to friends or relatives of the adjusters who received cash kickbacks.

Management discovered the scheme after one employee informed them that a co-worker had asked him to join the plot.

Industry: Transportation
Type: Travel advances never paid back
Amount: $120,000
Legal Action: Terminated, prosecuted, still in litigation
Perpetrator's Age: 45
Gender: Male
Length of Employment: 10 years

Fraud was committed by a subsidiary president who submitted a request for travel and entertainment advances without providing support. The chief accountant issued checks without advising anyone of the existing balance in the advance account. After one to one-and-a-half years, it was discovered that the president had not paid back the advances and could not support them with proper receipts. The matter is now pending in litigation.

Industry: Transportation
Type: Use of incoming check to purchase instrument later converted to cash
Amount: $20,000
Legal Action: None
Perpetrator's Age: 29
Gender: Male
Length of Employment: 6 years

The national company is a passenger carrier; one of its marketed products is "tailor-made" tours.

A routine tracing of an account receivable for several thousand dollars outstanding encompassing a seven months' period revealed that the amount had been paid in advance. As well as producing the cancelled check, the client indicated that it had been given to the tour clerk who had handled all of the arrangements. In the interim, the tour clerk had left the company's employ.

Investigation revealed that the tour clerk had used the check payable to the company to purchase a series of prepaid orders, a type of voucher which entitles the bearer to redeem it for any of the company's goods or services up to the amount shown on the face of the document. The perpetrator presented these prepaid orders to different cashiers over a period of several weeks and redeemed them for cash. Subsequent investigation proved that he had done this elsewhere.

Industry: Utility
Type: Collusion involving falsifying reports
Amount: $2,800
Legal Action: Terminated employee, prosecuted contractor
Perpetrator's Age: 27
Gender: Male
Length of Employment: 7 years

A contractor is hired annually to install gas mains in streets and services to individual homes. Billings to the utility company are based on square feet installed. A company inspector accompanies the contractor's crews to record the quantity of feet installed, and a copy of this report is sent to the contractor's office and used by him to prepare his invoice. The company uses the same report to verify its accuracy when received.

The contractor spent considerable time at the utility office. One day when the company distribution clerk responsible for verifying the contractor's invoice was away from his desk, the contractor handed him an envelope containing $50 with a note inscribed:

"Maybe you can do something for me sometime." Subsequently, the distribution clerk would insert a "1" in front of various numbers on the inspector's reports (i.e., 23 ft. would become 123 ft.). The contractor would then render his billing to include the additional footage added, as this report was used for both billing and verification purposes. Kickbacks were made to the company employee.

A polygraph test was utilized to obtain a confession from the employee and substantiate his story. The fraud was found by an internal auditor utilizing a record maintained by the engineering department.

Industry: Utility
Type: Consulting fee paid to steer business elsewhere
Amount: $150,000 +
Legal Action: Terminated
Perpetrator's Age: 55
Gender: Male
Length of Employment: 30 years

The vice president had considerable fiscal authorization and responsibility, and many administrative/operational departments reported to him. Using his authority, he steered construction work to a company in which he was an original incorporator and for which he was paid a consulting fee of $6,000 monthly. The company which employeed him full-time did business of approximately $3,000,000 over a three-to-four year period with the construction company which paid him for consulting.

Rumors of ". . . something is going on. . ." were pursued involving interviews both in and outside the company. Minutes of the construction company's board meetings documented the conflict of interest. The employee was terminated, and assets equal to the dollars paid to the vice president were written off.

Industry: Utility
Type: Double signing of employee-expense account checks by supervisor
Amount: $86,017
Legal Action: Terminated, prosecuted, incarcerated for 2 years
Perpetrator's Age: 57
Gender: Male
Length of Employment: 34 years

A young staff auditor was performing a routine accounts payable audit step of comparing payments to supporting documentation. A stratified statistical sample was employed in which only 1 percent of vouchers under $500 were selected for review. When the auditor couldn't find support for an employee-expense account payment, he asked how he could verify the appropriateness of the payment. The cancelled check paying the expense amount was examined for endorsements. It was double endorsed with one of the signatures being that of the accounts payable supervisor. Since the check was payable to an empoyee in a remote location and cashed in a local bank, there was no reasonable explanation. A quick search through the file of cancelled checks revealed other checks double endorsed with the accounts payable supervisor's signature. The payees were contacted, and it was learned that they had not received the proceeds and that their signatures had been forged.

The accounts payable supervisor was confronted and confessed to the embezzlement which totaled $87,000. Recovery was obtained from the company's Fidelity Insurance Bond. The accounts payable supervisor was prosecuted.

Industry: Utility
Type: Embezzlement of payments on account
Amount: $126,569
Legal Action: Terminated, prosecuted, sentenced to 2 years
Perpetrator's Age: 27
Gender: Female
Length of Employment: 6 years

Payments on accounts were embezzled as a result of customers' overpaying their utility bills. An employee cashed customers' checks at a local bank and took only the amount overpaid or cash out of daily collections.

Although the checks were made out to the company and restrictively endorsed, the bank still cashed the checks against the company's banking policy.

Industry: Utility
Type: Fraudulent payment of personnel payment fees
Amount: $83,000
Legal Action: Terminated, prosecuted, placed on probation
Perpetrator's Age: 33
Gender: Male
Length of Employment: 1 year

The personnel department is responsible for the initial processing and interviewing of applicants. Each applicant is required to complete an employment application form. One section relates to how the applicant became aware of the position: whether it was through an ad, a company acquaintance, or a placement agency.

After the initial interview by personnel wherein general company requirements and benefits are explained, the applicant is escorted to the appropriate location and supervisors for more interviews. If the applicant was sent through a placement agency and got the job, personnel was responsible for processing the firm's placement fee. The company location was not responsible for determining whether a placement agency had been used or the amount paid, even though they were charged for the expense.

A technical recruiter set up bogus placement agencies with different names by using initials, middle name, or combination of names and initials. When he interviewed applicants, he somehow persuaded the person to list one of his placement firms. The applicant was told that the placement firm was being used as a consultant and that the name had to be entered for identification. Applicants referred by employees were told that the reference did not look good on the application and that the applicant would have a better chance by using a placement firm's name. In both cases, the applicant was told there was no fee involved.

To make the agency appear authentic, someone would call the applicant and reinforce representations made by the recruiter. When an audit of the personnel department was performed, one procedure required the auditor to review hires made through outside placement agencies; and recent hires were selected for interviews. When asked about the use of placement agencies, some of the new hires revealed what had happened. A review of placement fees showed that they were processed and paid in many cases involving the technical recruiter. All hires by this recruiter were then interviewed. It was found that a number of fees had been improperly paid, amounting to an excess of $80,000. The recruiter was terminated and legal action was initiated. A bond claim was processed and the money recovered.

To eliminate the possibility of any recurrence, the following procedures were instituted. All placement agencies must provide information and references to personnel. Personnel verifies the information received and checks with the referenced companies regarding their experience with the agency. All placement agency payment requests must be to an approved agency and be initiated by the manager of personnel and initialed by the new hire and personnel director. Personnel must contact the supervisor over the new hire and verify that he/she is aware that the employee came through a fee agency and that the placement fee is to be charged to the location.

Industry:	Utility
Type:	Lapping cash receipts
Amount:	$173,000
Legal Action:	Terminated, prosecuted, trial pending
Perpetrator's Age:	31
Gender:	Female
Length of Employment:	5 years

Some daily cash payments received in the district office were held out of the daily bank deposits, and no entry was made on the company's books. When subsequent check payments were received from two large commercial customers, the previously unprocessed payment stubs were processed; and an equal amount was deducted from the commercial customer's payments. The effect was to show the embezzlement as a past-due balance on two large customers which had several separate accounts. The customers were the only ones to receive incorrect bills.

The same employee handled customers' bill complaints. She indicated that there was a computer problem which was being corrected and requested that they pay the current amount and ignore the past-due amounts.

This continued until the total due reached an age and amount that the division office requested the district office to take collection action. This required the employee to initiate unauthorized transactions by moving large amounts of money between accounts to clear the past-due amounts. These transactions came to the attention of management and triggered an investigation which determined that the company had suffered a loss in excess of $170,000.

Industry: Utility
Type: Lapping of customer payments
Amount: $129,000
Legal Action: Terminated, prosecution pending
Perpetrator's Age: 35 to 54
Gender: Female
Length of Employment: 6 to 14 years

Four clerks who had the joint responsibility for cash, accounts receivable, sales, opening the mail, and customer complaints acted in collusion to defraud the company of $129,000 by lapping accounts receivable and diverting sales proceeds to their personal use. One clerk kept books on the fraud so that accounts were not seriously delinquent.

The office had been audited four times during this period without detection of the fraud due to collusion. However, customer complaints to the home office prompted an investigative audit which discovered the embezzlement. Rotation of duties caused the "bookkeeper" to move out of the cash area. Another embezzler couldn't keep the "books" straight, causing customer complaints.

Industry: Utility
Type: Submission of copies of valid invoices for duplicate payments
Amount: $20,000
Legal Action: Terminated, turned over to district attorney
Perpetrator's Age: 38
Gender: Male
Length of Employment: 17 years

The project accountant was responsible for paying invoices for construction projects. This responsibility included coding invoices, obtaining approval for payment, preparing the voucher package, billing project owners for the invoice amounts, and issuing the checks. On two separate occasions, he copied invoices that were previously paid and issued duplicate checks. He took the checks and obtained an endorsement by a third party. The bank honored the checks which totaled approximately $20,000.

The fraud was discovered when a new employee noticed a duplicate vendor payment. When contacted, the vendor reported no knowledge of the duplicate payment as it had not been received. The internal audit department was called in at this point to determine what had happened, the extent of the problem, and if any similar occurrences had transpired. During the course of their research, internal audit found another duplicate payment made under the same set of circumstances. The project accountant was confronted and subsequently resigned. Documentation of the fraud was given to the district attorney's office for prosecution. Proceedings were also initiated to recover the misappropriated funds from the bank honoring the fraudulent endorsements. These funds were recovered, and the internal controls were strengthened in the department.

Industry: Utility
Type: Submission of fraudulent records
Amount: $3,200
Legal Action: None
Perpetrator's Age: 38
Gender: Male
Length of Employment: 7 years

After receiving a tip that someone had tried to launder a check drawn by a subsidiary, the records were reviewed and a voucher was found that had support documentation taken from the same month the prior year. The former year's original voucher contained a photocopy of the original delivery ticket. The coding/input form had been photocopied and altered, and the felt-tip writing looked amazingly original.

The A/P system audits for current year duplicates. All A/P employees were interviewed. The manager, who was questioned last, admitted "testing the system" just to see if his employees were observant. However, he couldn't remember what had happened to the check and said he had "forgotten" to reverse the entry from the accounting system.

The A/P manager was allowed to resign.

Industry: Utility
Type: Theft of petty-cash funds
Amount: $12,000
Legal Action: Terminated
Perpetrator's Age: 35
Gender: Male
Length of Employment: 7 years

Petty cash was in the custody of the head security officer. He had altered legitimate receipts to higher amounts – primarily for postage which is an overhead item and was loosely monitored. At a surprise count of the fund, only about $700 in currency and receipts were on hand of the $4,000 fund. Polygraph examinations were given to all security officers, but the head officer resigned before his test. A promissory note for the approximate $3,300 shortfall was executed by the terminated officer.

The Institute
of Internal Auditors
Research Foundation:1984-1985

The Institute
of Internal Auditors
International Research
Committee: 1984-1985

O. Jack McGill, Committee Chairman — Gulf Oil Corporation
Etienne Barbier — L'Oreal
Michael J. Barrett, DBA, CIA — University of Illinois at Chicago
Kenneth D. Carner, CIA — Security Pacific Corporation
John H. Cary, CPA — Price Waterhouse
Jennifer M. Fox, CIA — Southern Company Services
Arthur R. Gates, CIA, CPA — Norton Company
Joseph P. Greene — The Gillette Company
Michele Guenard, CPA — Peugeot Citroen
Arthur G. Heise — Bank Administration Institute
Keith R. Howe, DBA, CIA — Brigham Young University
James G. Johnston, CPA
Danny R. Kelly, CPA — Koch Industries, Inc.
Jean-Pierre Larrivee, CA — Metro-Richelieu, Inc.
Richard N. Lemieux, CPA — Ernst & Whinney
C. Richard McWilliams, CISA — Union Mutual Life Insurance
Company
Robert T. Mitchell — McIlwraith-Davey Industries, Ltd.
Lindsey S.W. Montgomery
Wayne G. Moore, CIA — Conoco, Inc.
Paul E. Nelson, CIA — 3M Company
Claire B. Nilsen — Wilmington Savings Fund Society
Frederick L. Page — Silver State Mining
James W. Pattillo, CMA, CPA — Indiana University
Walter D. Pugh, CDA, CISA, CPA — Price Waterhouse
Donald E. Ricketts, DBA — University of Cincinnati
David H. Rosenstein, CISA — Deloitte Haskins & Sells
Hanan Rubin, CIA — Metropolitan Life Insurance Company
Melvin F. Skindzier, CIA — JCPenney, Co., Inc.
Oscar Suarez, CIA, CMA — Great West Life Assurance Company
John P. Dattola — Staff Liaison of The Institute of Internal Auditors, Inc.